LETTER TO GOD

A Memoir:

Transcending Pain Through The Power Of Love

LETTER TO GOD

Marvin Lynn Faulkner

ISBN: 1082057746
ISBN 13: 9781082057748

DEDICATION

Letter To God is a gift from God. I dedicate it to God, family, and thousands of patients who daily suffer in pain. I have been blessed to comfort them. I have empathized and felt their pain. Love shared between us never failed to improve their individual condition. Love has never ceased to be the great healer allowing light to enter a world full of darkness and hatred.

Special thanks to my daughter Ali who never fails to get me to the finish line. To my son-in-law Bobby who's creative vision results in a book cover that is completely relevant. To Gentry, Taylor, and Zachary for their collective encouragement.

To Kathleen for revealing there is another survivor like myself with belief to endure and love rather than exist.

The struggle is real and it is LOVE that ensures not only a strong finish but a job WELL DONE!

TABLE OF CONTENTS

ACKNOWLEDGEMENTS

Unconditional love in my opinion is not a concept that is ever completely understood by the human race. No doubt we are overwhelmed with evidence of hatred in the world. We know love is present but not by watching the world news. I do believe people understand different levels of love. Unconditional love as given by the example of Christ is more likely absorbed into the soul of a human post suffering, pain, and loss. These emotions tend to strip the layers of self and replace them with tender mercies and less tendency to judge.

I have expressed much of this in my Letter To God. I think it important to mention a few of those who helped me understand this concept of unconditional love.

My mothers illness of the mind. My fathers humility. My wife's suffering and illness of the body. My children. Children contribute to the realization that self is not first. At least they should. Family and relatives that extended the hand of love during the most troubling of times. The handful of friends that remained such until death. Women that expressed any regard for me at all after my soul-mates death. Especially Kathleen whose own life dealt pain and loss allowing her to be respectful of mine. My last conversation with my cousin Tommy prior to his death has left an imprint that will not be forgotten. My uncle Shorty. I didn't fully comprehend it at the time. But something was different and I knew it. I am thankful I stood in his presence. To this day my Uncles stand out to me as people of inner strength and resolve framed by faith. Save one. He and my mother were mirror images as Tommy explained to me what I already knew before his death. Regardless we learned from them. I have also been blessed by having cousins that were more wonderful then I knew or could appreciate until I had suffered. John is suffering now but he will not one day. These cousins expressed such compassion and love to me when we were last together that I wept over the process. To my brother. Larry. I love you.

The thousands of patients that reminded me daily to realize that I had nothing complain about. For those of them who expressed their gratitude. For those that directed their hatred toward me when I had no choice but to follow the law.

Taylor. Ali. Gentry. I love you. Unconditionally.

To the parents of the mother of my children. Thank you for treating me like the son you never had. Despite myself.

There is not another that expresses unconditional love better than a devoted dog. I have been blessed to have some great ones. Two that will remain very special for the remainder of my days because they rescued me more than I did them.

My step-mother and her family that were so heavily needed to return the unconditional love of my father to me.

To my father in eternity that I look so forward to meeting. Finally I will understand everything. The Gift of living a life!!

The Gift! Life and everything I learned during the journey!

PROLOGUE

*The two most important days in your life are
the day you were born and the day you find
out why.*

—*Mark Twain*

There is a time to be born. A time to die. I have lived sixty-plus years. Did I believe I would live this long? For a time, I did not! For a time, I did not wish to. Did I have any idea what would come? Do I know how much longer I have? Surely not. I know death is inevitable.

This is my life. My letter to God. My account to submit to a higher being. The good, the bad, and the ugly. I believe if you read and accept the letter in part as your own, you will no longer be as concerned about death. We cling to life. It is natural—the instinct to survive.

Along the journey we can become so wrapped up in living that we don't prepare to die, so wrapped up in dying that we forget how to live. It comes from paralyzing fear. Fear of the unknown. The certainty of uncertainty.

Truth seems to rest on our ability to love, to give and receive it. There is no fear, shame, or regret in love. To discover this results in a more positive and peaceful existence. It can also allow death to be the beginning rather than the end. Love is the substance of all, the finality of everything that is!

CHAPTER 1

CHILDHOOD

Laying the foundation of life's house

You don't get to choose how you're going to die.
Or when.
You can only decide how you are going to live.
Now.

—*Joan Baez*

I was only a child, so what did I know? My world consisted of the trailer, my younger brother, Mom, Dad, Grandma (Mama), Grandpa (Papa), and me. Dad spent time coming and going in his fast Pontiac. He worked as an electrician in the steel mills of Indiana, and Mom was a beautician. Papa's farm was in Union City, Tennessee.

It was really hot in the summer. Mama and Papa lived in the farmhouse, and Mom, Dad, Larry, and I lived in a trailer next to the garden on a concrete pad. Every day Mama worked the garden, and I helped her haul potatoes to the basement. That wasn't why I loved the garden. It was because of the summer cabbage and tomatoes. At six years old, I found peace and joy in washing these items while eating them beneath a peach tree. For a time, I knew what it was to be truly happy. It was a contest between the sun and my smile as I ate a better meal than any diner could offer. I didn't start my life seeking to be unhappy.

Dad came home on the weekend from work. He left so quickly I hardly knew he was there. He and Mom fought bitterly during these times. I didn't know why. I know now. The cabbages, tomatoes, and water hose used to wash the vegetables were my escape from the confusion. I found peace, at least for a moment in time.

Breakfast at Mama's table, with eggs and biscuits, was always good. I liked the bacon. I also liked watching Papa sopping up the bacon grease with a biscuit. He poured his hot coffee into a saucer and drank it after he blew on it a few times. I was too young for coffee, according to Mama's rules. I wanted breakfast to last all day because it was quiet. There was no fighting! I liked my eggs and gravy. With a nod of Papa's head, however, it was over. Time to join him for the chores.

The barn was not large, as I look back, but to a six-year-old, it seemed huge. Stall after stall were lined up on both sides of the barn. It smelled of oil from the tractor and poop from the cows. The piles of hay and the sharp tools near bales of wire were a chamber of horrors, yet I followed Papa inside without fear. He lined the big beasts up and squeezed their tits until the white cream came. He taught me the art of squeezing tits and filling buckets.

Papa was very mischievous. My brother was three years younger than I, but he followed along sometimes. Papa persuaded him to pull on one of the calves' balls before they were cut. The calf kicked him to the other side of the barn! It was cold, my brother had on a thick coat, and it was just a calf, so he wasn't hurt. Papa laughed. Most likely that would not be considered funny these days.

We poured the cream from the buckets into big metal containers and took the containers to the gravel road in front of the house, where the dairy company Papa did business with picked them up. At breakfast I always had a glass of cold milk, and Mama made sure we knew it was from the effort of milking cows.

After the milking, it was time to take the tractor ride to the fields, where there were rows and rows of white cotton balls. The group of small farm dogs and the larger collie always followed. I enjoyed the dogs and, of course, can remember each one and his or her name to this day. Papa favored Bounce, the collie. Bounce had fought with many critters of the night through the years. With his thick hair, he usually came out the winner. The hair made Bounce harder to bite. He was very territorial and would not tolerate dogs from other farms coming around without a fight. I saw old Bounce run off big, tough-looking dogs. He would chase them until they were both out of sight. After a while Bounce would return and lie down and rest. Papa would smile, walk by, and give him a pat on the head.

Soon we would take the sacks off the wagon and start picking cotton. Papa would make a bet with me that I couldn't out-pick him, and being just a kid, I never had a chance, but I would try. Every now and then, I would think my bag was getting heavy, and Papa would laugh. I'd turn around, and Teddy and Penny, the little dogs, would be lying on my sack as I was dragging it along. They looked for every opportunity to get on my sack, and it would make me mad, but it seemed to be fun for Papa.

We would work all morning and sometimes a little into the afternoon, but when it got too hot, Papa would call it off to head back and do other chores. Once a week we'd go to the mill and deliver our cotton. Papa would get paid a little, and he usually would sit me down at the diner and buy me a chocolate milk and a candy bar. Papa was a hard worker, and this was during the 1950s and '60s when small farmers were still around and could make a living if they owned their land and houses. I can say I picked cotton in the field. Roy Clark had a song called "I Never Picked Cotton," but I sure as heck did.

Mama supported the farm by working in town for a company where she sewed all day. The name was Slant and Slant. Mama was a hard worker as well. How she could keep up with the needs of the farm, Papa, and me while holding yet another job I couldn't appreciate— not until I did something similar as an adult.

Before I knew it, summer was over, and it was time for me to go back to school. At almost seven, I moved up to second grade. I saw Papa only at the breakfast table. Mama made the gravy so good! She would put it over toast and crumble boiled egg over it for me. Papa's eggs were over medium, and he had his biscuits to sop up the bacon grease. Mama let me know when it was time to go stand at the gravel road and wait for the bus. She usually gave me a hug and kiss, but not before she stuck her false teeth out at me. She liked to scare me that way. I would say goodbye and walk out to take my place by the metal milk jugs. Before long the bus would crest the hill and come to a quick stop, and I would hop on.

This was our routine then: Dad running the roads back and forth from the steel mills of Indiana, Papa heading to the barn in the morning, and me getting on the bus in the morning and then getting off the bus in the afternoon at Mama's house while Mom was at beautician school. I will never know why it changed one day. I did gather that Crabtree, the bus driver, never liked me. He was always staring at me. I tried hard to convince myself it wasn't true. Regardless, I was scared of him, but I never said anything about it.

It all came to a head one day. I was standing by the milk jugs as usual, and Crabtree pulled up, slowed down...and left me! I became filled with the fear of God Almighty! I knew I was in trouble, for there would be no choice but to tell Mama and face Papa. You see, I had heard things about Papa: that he could be a mean, ill-tempered man. He and Uncle Claude were part Indian, and you could see it more in Claude than Papa, but Papa's reputation was known over the county hills. I had never seen him explode with temper. I never wanted to.

So I went to Mama and said, "He left me, Mama."

She took off her apron and said, "Well, I'll have to get Papa."

Soon he came and pulled the old pickup truck out from the garage. I jumped in and didn't say a word. Papa let me out at school and said, "Boy, don't let that happen again."

I didn't say anything. I just ran to my classroom, traumatized. I had a hard time doing my lessons all morning. At lunchtime they served banana pudding, so that calmed me down. I loved banana pudding so much that I didn't care that Mrs. Pepper scolded me for licking the bowl. She was a sweet teacher, and she favored good manners. Licking the bowl wasn't considered mannerly.

When I got off the bus at home, Mom would get home shortly afterward. Until then I got to run and play with the dogs and feed them. When Mom came home,

I would run to her, hug her, and say hello. I would later greet Mama and Papa once we went inside the farmhouse. Sometimes Mama would show me where she had hidden her precious Dr Peppers and give me one. We usually ate supper at Mama's house, and Mom would help her cook. I had many a good chicken dinner then, even though watching Mama wring the birds' necks and pluck their feathers wasn't as enjoyable as eating them.

The next morning, I was standing by the milk jugs, and I couldn't believe it. Crabtree did it again! He pulled up, slowed down, and left me. I stood there frozen in fear. I believed Papa would whip me. I saw a ruffling of the living room curtains. Mama came out, with Papa right behind her, and said, "Come on, child. Papa was watching and saw the whole thing."

Papa started the old truck and said, "Get in, son."

I couldn't get in fast enough; my bag of books and lunch pail were airborne along with my little body. The only thing Papa said was, "I used to drive the school bus, and I know the route."

Over the gravel roads we went as fast as the truck could go. As I held on for dear life, we saw the bus. Papa cut Crabtree off at a fork in the road. Both the truck and the bus came to a sudden stop, and Papa said, "Follow me, boy."

I got out, and when Papa got to the door of the bus, Crabtree was holding on to the lever, yelling, "Mr. Taylor, I didn't mean anything by it! I was just fooling around."

Papa kicked the door in, and the handle jerked out of Crabtree's hand. Papa went in, and he hit the young man, slapping him so many times while Crabtree cried for him to stop. He said, "I promise, Mr. Taylor, I'll never leave him again."

Papa kept on slapping him. The other children were mortified. I was in shock. Finally, Papa stopped and said, "Leave him again, you bastard, and see what happens!"

Crabtree said, "I won't, Mr. Taylor. I swear to God I won't."

Papa turned to me and said, "Now, get on the bus, son."

I jumped in, and Papa drove away. Crabtree wiped off his blood and snot with a rag, and there was not a sound to be heard on the bus. He never left me again, nor did he ever even look at me. What happened that day was never talked about, never brought up. I guess that was the way things were handled in those days. Not today!

Looking back, I know there had to be some bad blood between Papa and Crabtree. All I know is that after this, the story I had heard about my papa nearly beating a man to death with a hammer in a hardware store seemed believable. I knew Papa was in his sixties— not that I knew what that meant, but it seemed old. And I thought old men didn't beat up younger men. When I was six and seven, that seemed to be my limited under-standing. I learned a lesson that day. There are rage, youth, experience, and downright meanness, but I will never forget this one thing: Papa slapped the shit out of young Crabtree.

So there it is and was: growing up in the South. Mom, Dad, Larry, Mama, Papa, and the farm. The dogs and cows, milk and cotton, summer tomatoes and cabbage, a garden hose. The bus and Crabtree, old Papa, his hot coffee from the saucer, the bacon grease, the truck and gravel, and yeah, the banana pudding. I stopped licking the bowl. Mrs. Pepper told me she would whip me if I did. I was on my way to the art of learning about life and love. I had a long way to go. My introduction to life was a combination of great happiness, the dogs and cows, milk and cotton, interrupted with moments of terror, like Crabtree. Love was there, lurking beneath the shadows of tough resolve.

We all have our early years. Mine are mine—better than some and worse than others. I didn't share them to bore or enlighten you. It was only to suggest that I had a start, just like you. Many times this beginning is what forms us, causes us to choose what we do, to react to blessings as well as hardships in the manners we were taught. A lifetime taught at the beginning of things.

These are the things I remember. This is my beginning. It was humble enough. It was not long, even in these early years, before I understood I was not born into material wealth. Any fame or fortune that might come would be from my own efforts and positioning in time.

I would ask you to pause. Think of your childhood. Understand it is what it is. It was what it was. Despite your understanding or lack thereof, you lived through it. You are what you are. If you like yourself, most likely you have navigated the waters of childhood successfully. When you gaze into a mirror, it is important that you like and accept what you see. In a healthy way, love what you see! This love explains your ability to accept the past—the good, the bad, and the ugly. If you don't like or love yourself yet? If it has anything to do with the past? Let it go. You cannot change it. Forgive yourself. Forgive others. Do this so you can love. Do this so you can live. Fully! Care enough about yourself and others to do this. Care enough to let yesterday go. Live completely in the only thing you have: the here and now! That's not easy to do at times. The alternative of bitterness and hatred doesn't help.

I struggle with this every day: attempting to look ahead and not behind. Spending time in the past is looking into the rearview mirror. I have an inner since of loss and sadness due to regret: Another path. A different direction. The belief that other choices would have made a difference, that I would have been better off. That is a falsehood, for there is no way of knowing how a different choice would have turned out. This is not healthy. The front windshield of a car is larger, as it is meant to view the present and future: full of adventure, opportunity for growth, and the chance to apply wisdom from the teachings and lessons of the past.

There was and is no control over your childhood: How you were raised. The positives. The negatives. You work with what you were given. If it was harsh, look at it. Don't bury it but rather accept it. You now have control of your adulthood. Choose to be different! Choose love.

The kindness and softer love you learn creates your ability to love and offer tender compassion and mercy. We redirect any negative to the positive and bathe daily in the positives that we are given. After all, we have been given the gift of life. It is our choices in handling the uncertainty of life that will frame us.

Let us choose the light of love, to the best of our abilities.

CHAPTER 2

GROWTH
Expanding and adapting the foundation

We do not see things as they are,
we see them as we are.

—Anaïs Nin

The day came when Mom was done with beautician school, and Dad was tired of driving all weekend from work and back. Dad moved us to Indiana. A few years had passed since my beginnings on the Tennessee farm. Times were good, it seemed, for working people in the 1960s. We had a new trailer and new car. Mom and Dad seemed to be all right for the most part. My little brother and I were doing OK. There were times when Larry and I seemed closer then, but it was not to last. I always thought I was a good older brother, but

I would live to see the day when he didn't share those feelings. Our relationship would end painfully, but that explanation is for a little further down the road.

Mom believed I was destined to become a concert pianist. Beginning in the fourth grade, when I got home from school, I was always practicing. My brother would run and hide because he knew what would happen if I hit a wrong note. Mom might warn me once, but after that I was whipped with a belt. The sad thing was Mom believed if one of us got punished, the other should as well. Even though my brother was spoiled and selfish in my opinion, he was only a little boy. He didn't deserve getting whipped when I hit a wrong note. I don't know what ever made Mom think this was right. I knew she loved us, but this behavior mystifies me to this day. All I can remember is my little brother screaming, "I didn't do anything. He hit the wrong note." But there it was: the belt and two screaming kids, the whipping, my brother's look of disgust with me. Each time this repetitive theme was concluded, I returned to the piano with efforts not to make mistakes.

I don't know where Mom found my piano teacher, Mrs. Hill. She was about as stern as my mom. She didn't whip me or anything like that. Mom felt that was her duty and hers alone. Mother would beat the shit out of anyone else who touched us. I lived to witness that on two occasions. Once was when she slapped a teacher of mine for disciplining me and the rest of the classroom for what two other boys had done. Another was when she saw a neighborhood bully hit me with a bullwhip. Mother beat him all the way back to his trailer and threatened to do the same to his mother.

After Mom whipped us, she would say, "If that doesn't do it, then I'll tell your dad." As a result, we lived in morbid fear of our dad during those early years, because if he had something worse waiting, we wanted no part of it.

Mrs. Hill did have a ruler, though, and every time I did something wrong, she would stomp her feet and hit my hand with the ruler. Mom seemed to think that was fine. I guess it's obvious why it didn't take long for me to get good at playing the piano. I won some regional competitions, and I was the star of most recitals. I hit the notes with precision and accuracy. I was well on my way to being what my mom dreamed of, a concert pianist.

There are beginnings and ends to all things, and this was no exception. I sat through lesson after lesson with Mrs. Hill, her ruler, and her stomping feet. Most of Mom's whippings had stopped by the time I was in junior high. She thought slaps across the face were good enough at that age. At least my brother was relieved the punishment had been reduced to that. Maybe it was those days that caused him to resent me. Perhaps that was why he believed I owed him. Then again, he seemed to believe my parents owed him as well. In part this was due to his idea that I was somehow loved more than he.

For one larger recital, several hundred people were packed into a Methodist church in Northeast Indiana.

Students were being groomed for bigger things to come regarding music. When it was my turn, I turned to my brother and said, "Watch this, little brother." I wish I had never said that. I got up, walked confidently through the crowd, and took the seat at the grand piano. I positioned my hands and started my Chopin concerto. It flowed without pause, and I got conceited enough to move a little with the music, as if the music was from the heart. It wasn't. It was simply a technical masterpiece bought with pain, a ruler, whippings, and my brother's cries for mercy.

My hands were positioned perfectly, and I was more than halfway through the concerto when I smiled and thought, *This is mine. I paid for it, and now everyone will watch the technician at work.* I was already preparing for the bow, the prideful, arrogant smile, the walk back, and sitting there with everyone saying, "There he is… the new Mozart" (even though I was playing Chopin).

Then it happened. I was looking around, not focusing on the keys because of my confidence, when I saw it. On the sill of the stained-glass window was a sparrow, a cute little bird just sitting there looking at me. Like a zoom lens on a camera, it seemed, I instantly turned him into a condor. I could see all of him. Every feather. I stopped playing. I looked down at the keys. My hands were not there! I was just sitting there. Close to a thousand people, including Mrs. Hill, my mom, my dad, and my brother, were all waiting—plus the sparrow and me. I was hypnotized.

The stomping of Mrs. Hill's foot brought me out of it. The entire audience was completely silent. I looked out and saw my dad. He was looking at me as if he thought the song was over. My mom, on the other hand, was sinking slowly into her seat. My brother was mortified and most likely concerned this would lead to yet another beating.

Mrs. Hill said, "Start over."

I looked to the window, and the sparrow flew away. I was horrified, reduced to a cowardly junior high kid who felt like running. But I couldn't move my feet, so I started over.

As the fear started to leave, all I wanted to do was finish. I played faster and faster. I was going to get this nightmare over with! No more timing, just fingers flying across the keyboard. I turned this classic into a Jerry Lee Lewis "Great Balls of Fire." I swear I could see the keys flying through the air and then falling down in time for me to hit them again—keys flying and my fingers trying to keep up the pace.

Within an instant I was at the same place where I had stopped before. I said in my mind, *Not this time. Go right through it and finish this disaster.* It was not to be, however. It happened again. The blackout. My hands wouldn't go. I could not remember the music. I knew what to do this time. I continued. I had no idea what I was playing. With a chord and run from one end of the keys to the other, I finished it. I leaped off the bench and started my brisk walk back to my seat. As I went by Mrs. Hill, she said sarcastically, "Well, I don't know what that was!" I passed my mother, who was slumped down in the church pew.

I sat down next to my brother. He said, "Well, you really showed them. Thanks a lot!"

Others still had to play. I sat there waiting for hell, waiting in agony for the trip to the car and the pain that would follow. When we finally left, my brother and I sat in the back of the family's new Pontiac, and no one spoke for a while. Then, out of nowhere, I said, "Mom, I will never play again! Do you understand? I'm sick of it. I won't play, and you can't make me!"

My brother was horrified, worried that Mom would kill us both, but for some reason I was not. I knew this was some sort of milestone in my life. I couldn't explain it. I had no idea where my sudden courage had come from. I was starting the journey into manhood, a time of reckoning that there was one life and one chance. I was not going to live mine like this.

My mom turned and said, "You listen to me. Don't tell me—" My brother flinched, and I waited for the slap. But all I heard was my dad. Maybe he was tired of the times he'd sat in his car with the heater running in those harsh Indiana winters, waiting for me to finish my lessons with Mrs. Hill. Maybe he thought of the time my mom had gone to school to pick me up for a lesson only to find out Mrs. Baker was keeping the class after school because two of the class clowns, Chris and Doug, had been caught playing with an electrical cord and outlet. I remember my mom knocking on the door and asking why in the hell I was being held late. The answer didn't suit her, and Mrs. Baker soon realized she had tangled with an insane woman. My mom dragged me from the classroom while Mrs. Baker ran for her life. Perhaps Dad knew it had gone on long enough. All I know is he never said much to Mom when it came to us. This time he did. He said, "Joanne, leave the boy alone!"

My mom knew by his tone that my dad would beat her if she didn't listen. He had before. So she turned around. That was the end of it. No more lessons. No more pain from the piano. My brother had finally escaped. The rest of the ride home was quiet.

A few years passed. I did play again, but only to accompany Mom when she sang in church. She had a beautiful voice. No more recitals just hymns such as "Just a Closer Walk with Thee," "Amazing Grace," "In the Garden," and others. There came a day when she selected "His Eye Is on the Sparrow." She never knew it, but I had a hard time getting through that one. I left the church, went out back, and laughed my ass off.

Those were the days in Indiana—the steel mills, the Pontiac, junior high, and the piano. The time my eye was on the sparrow and the changes it brought. We have all hit wrong notes because of our choices. I remember thinking, even that early in life, that youth didn't give me the wisdom to choose carefully, and I foolishly thought there was plenty of time for me to find myself. So I ventured forth into the nights and days filled with the only real truth: the certainty of uncertainty. Pain and life. Lessons harsh and without mercy. The love I knew in the early years was tough yet tender in a strange way. Looking back, I know it was complex and not easy to comprehend.

No matter your experience, do you remember the first time you stood against the wind of change? The day you fought to belong to yourself, to take a stand, and the hope that came with it? From that point I knew I would stand and fight for the right to choose. Later I learned the right to choose comes with the right to choose well or poorly, the right to make mistakes. Our failure to believe that mistakes are inevitable can result in our inability to forgive ourselves. This results in increased fear. There is no love in fear, not for ourselves or anyone else. What I share with you is not out of pride, arrogance, pity, conceit, sorrow, or any other minor or major note. It is solely out of love, with the hope you will recall your own experience.

Recently I sat on a bench in the River Market park in Kansas City observing a homeless man playing a community piano. He played Mozart's Piano Sonata no. 16 in C Major and Beethoven's "Moonlight Sonata." I had played both decades before. His performance was technically sound. Afterward, I approached him to tell him how I appreciated his effort. He indicated he had been playing for only four years. He added he wished he had started sooner. I told him I had, and we were both in the same place.

His smile revealed the poor condition of his teeth. I asked if he needed anything, and he replied, "Something to eat." I gave him twenty dollars. After thanking me, he walked away. While walking home, I was reminded of the irony in life. I was thankful for the opportunity to love in this situation. I ask you again to collect your thoughts. Choose to fight for change. In the end, please understand that less is in fact more! Despite having more or less, we all end up in the same place. The homeless man and I experienced different journeys. We did not share everything in common. Nor do you and I. The stranger did play the piano as well as I ever did. He loved himself enough to take time to play. In his case, I believe the music set him free. This same music imprisoned me. The difference? Fear versus love. I could hear love in his music. I am confident there was fear in mine. Which would you rather hear? The sound of love is all around us, in the present. If I can hear it, so can you. The homeless man does. Our paths may be rocky. Heartaches are certain. As for me, I will leave this world believing that love is our friend!

I have always preferred Beethoven over Mozart and Chopin. I now understand why. For the first time, I play the piano with love, compassion, and yet pain. Not fear, however. Such is life. People who listen when I play say they can hear all of these emotions in my music. I am not Beethoven, but now I can hear and feel him. I can say I understand his pain and his losses regarding love.

Life demands changes. Constantly. Nothing remains the same. We must adapt and have the courage to change with the ebb and flow of life. We expect the fastball only to be thrown a curve. In an instant we are required to adjust. Do we give up? Surrender? It must be our tough resolve to step up to the plate again, to plant our feet. We do not satisfy ourselves with the agony of defeat. Rather we accept the challenge and persuade ourselves to try again—to obtain the will to survive and utilize the pain to push us onward.

I was taught to live life with paralyzing fear. Today, however, I choose to live life with unconditional love. Love casts out fear. I would be a liar if I told you that fear does not return and torment me. I do, however, fight it. In many cases I win. I only do so when I utilize love.

CHAPTER 3

CHANGES
The right to remodel

Life is like a piano.
What you get out of it depends on how you
play it.

—*Tom Lehrer*

From the trailer to our first house, things seemed to be going well for a while. It was time for me to decide what I was going to do. Now that the piano had been put to rest, I desired to be a part of the norm rather than the exception. Baseball became my answer. I was better at it than I expected. The discipline I had been taught from the piano, added to my natural athletic ability, was to my advantage. I didn't become good out of fear but rather love. I loved to play baseball. Soon I was an all-star shortstop on the summer Optimist league. I was the leadoff hitter. I almost never failed to get on base. My strike zone was small. If I didn't walk, it was a base hit or double to right center. I was fast. Stealing a base was not a problem.

Our family relocated once again. The move ended my baseball career. As I reached the end of junior high, I was ready to try out for the high school team. The new school was about thirty miles outside of Chicago. The tryout never happened. I had not grown much physically up to that time. My short and small stature resulted in my first real rejection. The head baseball coach took one look at me and said, "You must be joking. You're not big enough to play." He would not even let me put on my glove for an official tryout.

Things like this can alter youth and the chances it offers forever. I never believed it was right, but the years since have taught me not much is.

The only thing the coach did offer was a question: "Do you know how to wrestle?" My answer was no. He directed me to a sport defined by weight classes, where there was room for "little guys."

My Dad was bigger than I even after I was grown. His side of the family did have some larger men, and my mom had a couple of brothers who made good-sized uncles. It was my fate that I was to take after my mom, and small is what I was. It occurred to me that my small stature was a test. How would I deal with it? After all, isn't that the key to most things?

I must say that during that time, other things happened that took precedence over my pain surrounding baseball. My grandmother died in her sleep. My mom changed after that. She already had problems. Her lack of management regarding Mama Ali's death added to them. Further depression sank in. The problems between her and Dad got worse. The short time of peace in our home was over.

After her mother's death, I witnessed things between Mom and a couple of her siblings that were terrible. There was fighting over material possessions, the things that make life seem trivial and small. It was ugly. How do we place such importance on things that in the end will be sold at a garage sale, with few understanding why they should offer more than a dollar? Anyway, it happened, and I watched it. I did not understand. I now see that these types of things can frame our experiences and create bitterness that can linger for years. How much better would our lives be if we could grasp the perspective that less is more before old age creeps in?

I started wrestling right away. The rest of the team members had been learning the sport for a few years. I had to make up ground quickly. Tenth grade found me learning the basic wrestling techniques. When I was a junior, I went undefeated on the junior varsity mat. Senior year gave me my chance on the varsity team. I set a school and state record for takedowns. Our team was ranked first in the state. Still, with all the champions on that team, I remained the untested weak link in the chain.

The biggest obstacle I faced was my slow development in maturing physically. Other guys were shaving and such, but not me. There was no need. My quickness was not a problem. Although strong, I became much stronger quickly after my high school graduation.

I did well, but not like I could have if I had been stronger earlier. I won over thirty wrestling matches and lost only four, including my junior varsity record. I can say no one ever beat me twice. Whatever I did wrong I corrected. I never had a lopsided match. My losses were 1–0, 7–6, 4–2, and 3–0, with one draw (9–9). One of the losses and the draw I avenged. I won against the 7–6, 5–3. The 9–9 I later bested 9–5.

I never wrestled badly except for the 3–0. My opponent in that match wrestled very well. For some reason my timing was off. I never got into a rhythm. I did have him turning over to his back when time ran out, but the match got away from me. I remember my uncle was there. I looked up and saw him right before I walked on the mat. I loved him. I remember thinking, I have to wrestle well. I wanted him to see me at my best.

I have to say, though, that was likely the worst performance I ever rendered. The combination of an excellent effort from the opponent, whom I should have beaten, and a horrible one from me led to that loss. Perhaps I placed too much pressure on myself, or an element of fear crept in. I can't say for sure.

I don't think I ever would have lost to any of my opponents twice except possibly one. This opponent had been to state competition before and was simply technically better than I. Not by much, though. Clayton was very skilled. My loss to him was rather confusing. With time running out, I believed I had skillfully executed a takedown and would be awarded two points and the victory. The official determined I didn't have complete control of Clayton, and as he maneuvered around me the official awarded him two points at the sound of the buzzer. The 4–2 victory was his in a matter of a heartbeat.

Even to this day, I remember most of my opponents, though time can dilute memories. In the end, despite winning the conference championships and sectional and regional semifinals, I lost my bid to go to state as described above. In years to follow, the rules were changed, allowing the first four regional finalists to take the state trip. During my years, only the regional champ was given this opportunity.

The thing I remember most about wrestling was what the coach said to me in the locker room after my final match, an 8–3 victory over what had been an undefeated opponent for much of the season. He said, "If I knew you were going to be this good, I would have worked with you harder." He was a difficult man, and back then was a different day. He was a coach who didn't mind slapping the crap out of you for a mistake—something I was more than accustomed to. Still, he was an excellent coach, and although we didn't end up taking the state title, we went the season undefeated in team competition. There were our individual scores and records. Then there was our combined team record. This team record was the reason we were ranked number one in the state before the actual state competition. The funny thing that took place in the locker room while Coach Johnson was giving me this moment of tenderness was what was going on in my mind. I was thinking of baseball—how much I had missed playing it!

Fate was not kind, not only for me, but for our entire team. We all fell at the end. I think it was mainly because of the officials' hatred of our coach. Anything close did not go our way. Even those on our team who were undefeated lost in the regionals. Only three of the magnificent thirteen made it through to the state level. One got beat in his first match at state. The other two took second, and we ended up in sixth place as a team.

One of the best days of my life was when I wrestled my way into a championship bout in a tournament. My opponent for the finals was undefeated. He was bigger and stronger, and most people didn't give me much of a chance. On the night of the tournament, the gym in Hobart, Indiana, was full, and the noise was deafening. Our team peaked a little too soon. Everyone made it to the finals. It seemed like a regular meet rather than a tournament as my teammates and I lined up across from our opponents from several different schools. It was amazing!

My time came. My two teammates before me won, and I was riding high with emotion. Adrenaline coursed through my blood. The match started, and immediately I felt my opponent's strength. He grabbed my neck and tossed me to the mat like a rag doll. I fought with him like this for the first two periods, struggling to be free and reacting to being tossed around as if I were nothing. Everything was happening fast, and he was ahead 2–1. I wondered how I had managed to keep it that close.

With less than a minute left in the match, I felt him give. His strength was not the same, and his breathing was heavy. I looked at him, and his eyes seemed dazed and confused. I realized he was tired, and I wasn't. To this day I can still hear the screams of almost a thousand people. I looked at the clock, and there were twenty seconds left. Then ten. My arms found his legs, and I pulled and turned. He was down, and I was in control. I heard the referee say, "Two points," as the buzzer sounded. It was ironic that my bid for the state title was ended in the same way with the tables being turned as I described.

I won this one, however. I remember running around like one of Mama's headless chickens. I raised my hands in the air, and the referee grabbed my raised arm to confirm I was the champion. He handed me my trophy, and my eyes landed on my parents and brother, who were standing and applauding. Tears rolled down my dad's face; my mom was screaming with joy (rather than the anger I had heard all my life). My brother was jumping up and down. I sprinted up the bleachers, handed my father the trophy, and kissed and hugged them all. My tears mixed with theirs, and for the first time in my life, I felt important and loved. I had pleased my folks. Even my brother was happy!

A few weeks later, when I lost my bid for the state title, I was alone. I ended up in third place in the regional qualifier, and my family left before my match for third. No one in my family stayed to support me in my defeat before the consolation match. I returned to the place inside that's reserved for pain: that place within the heart where blood carries life and death; the place known as heartache and hurt, with the reminder that, like a breeze, happiness can come to an end. I learned every victory should be celebrated, but losses teach us so much more about integrity, patience, endurance, and even love. For that reason, we should embrace the losses and not fear them.

Of the first four contestants on my old team, I believe I am the only one still alive. One died of a drug overdose, another was run over and killed while he was walking in the road drunk, and the other fought alcoholism. I saw him over two decades ago. He was not well. I tried to stay in contact with him despite his problem, but I had my hands full raising my children. Over time I lost contact and am not sure what happened to him. The days spent striving for excellence on the mat didn't translate to the same desire in life for the others as it did for me.

A few weeks prior to my disappointment regarding the end of my wrestling days, Papa had another stroke.

Mom, the youngest of his nine children, refused to send him to a nursing home. He came to live with us during my last couple of high school years and was moved into my room. Dad worked the steel mills. Coming home to Papa's impaired condition did not help Dad's relationship with Mom. The added strain on an already-weakened union was the beginning of the end. I looked with sadness at the old man I had picked cotton with, who had rescued me from the bus driver. He could no longer speak and was dependent on us. So while I struggled on the wrestling mat, there was another, more powerful battle going on at home.

Even through the dementia Papa eventually developed, the old farmer remained. At times he strayed from the house and urinated on the sidewalk, as though he were still on the farm. On a few trips to the grocery store before his dementia and physical conditioned worsened, he would tease and nudge me every time a large woman walked by. Papa always liked the larger ones! Unfortunately, his end came harshly, and it was not easy to watch. I was told Papa was dying, and my choice was to go compete in a wrestling match or stay home. There was nothing I could do, and Dad thought I should go. The result was a 1–0 loss because all I could think of was Papa and his suffering. I barely noticed my opponent, though I felt him.

After it was over, my coach took me aside and informed me that my grandpa had passed. I went to the locker room and wept. I didn't care about the match. My guilt for not holding the hand of the man I had picked cotton with and who had taught me how to milk a cow was more than I could bear. His passing was the wrestling match I wish I would have attended, not the one I went to. I was just a kid and in many ways not even a young man, but I became one that day—the day I first knew what was important in life and what wasn't. In my mind, I deserved to lose, for I already had. The thought would follow me for many days to come. Despite these feelings, I finished the wrestling season as strong as I could. I did this to honor Papa as well as myself.

As I stated, the confusion of Papa living and dying at our house would spell the end for my mother and. Papa's death was the final straw. It was the end of wrestling in more than one way, and the match between my parents would end in a draw, one that would haunt my brother and me for life. I will not forget wrestling on the mat, but I will remember the matches off the mat more: the fine line between victory and loss; the close relationship between them. I believe they come together. One is not complete without the other, like. Like a torrid love affair that loses the flame and is then rekindled—the waves of the sea and life, forever to break against the sands of time. I was to learn more about love and what really mattered. About walls that are supposed to protect yet imprison us. Using fear, engaging it, letting it guide us. Turning curses into challenges. The emotions of living in a world such as this.

I went back after graduation and worked out with the team a few times. I had no trouble with any of them who were near my weight. My additional year of physical maturity made the difference. Another of life's lessons: timing is everything.

High school offered up one more thing I really did enjoy. Despite my troubles with the piano, it wasn't hard for me to be good on a small combo organ. A few guys and I formed a band. We didn't turn out too bad. We played for a couple of dances and were known as a cover band. In other words, we didn't write our own songs but played everything from pop to rock—good stuff to dance to. This was a fun time in school. We were asked to warm up the crowd for another band at the Sherwood Club in Indiana. They were unknown at the time but not for long. They turned out to be on their way to becoming Styx!

Naturally, making it to the big time isn't easy. How many of us wish we could have been a part of the Eagles? My band was yet another short stop on my way to becoming a physician. Without a doubt, it was fun. Yet it was one more turn in life off the straight path, down a gravel road. There is little doubt the gravel can be slippery and rough. Yes, there are even holes big enough to flatten a tire. Isn't it ironic that, when years have passed and we look back, we welcome that gravel? The clean paved road may have been safer, but in so many ways, it was sober and boring as hell. Surrendering one's creativity is not cheap. Not at all. My God, what a price to pay for safety. I understand it. Everyone needs to eat. Not all see gold or platinum. I have been given to wonder, though, as long as there is a roof and a meal, how many long for the gravel? For a road that demands the creative process to continue and improve? My hat is off to those who would rather die than give up on a dream or desire.

I remember the applause, the dancing onstage and off, the girls screaming for another tune. Our drummer and the trumpet player. I remember the guitars. They offered up enough that we sounded good, even if we were put to shame by a couple of longhairs who came over and blasted out Led Zeppelin. They shook the house down. It wasn't long before my mom had them out the door. With my luck they probably were future hall of famers on their way to LA.

The music of the band concluded. The chorus of life continued. Sometimes it was a church choir that sounded like angelic manifestation. Other times it was a quartet made up of four deaf-mutes attempting to grunt in harmony. I cry out, Lord! How strange is this place between heaven and hell? How many times, whether to a god or not, depending on your faith, have you cried out to anyone or anything that might listen? Why do we cry out this way? Both you and I do it.

I think most of us are searching for answers as to the why and what for. Most of us gain some peace in understanding that there isn't much that's understandable here. Rather accept that there are reasons for things. Deeply appreciate that hope for clarity ends in confusion. It will be death that frees us, no matter the quality of life or the lack of glamor.

I have noted many a scholar proclaiming that our successes and failures here are mere matters of perception. I understand this. Early in life I was taught fear in many different forms. For the most part, I have concluded this emotion doesn't serve us well. It became a fight through the years, a fight not to be afraid.

What perceptions do you have? If you have fear, my friend, you are not alone. I share these stories and more for no other reason than to encourage you to continue fighting for the right to remain and love while here. The right to make a difference in your life and the life of others. When you choose to love, the difference is evident. Lives are changed forever by the love you give and share. It's better to share love than fear. I know I feel better during times of love verses moments of morbid fear.

Not long ago I cried out in the dark of night again. There was no one present but the dogs and me, considering the physical. With faith, however, I believe that a universe, a god, a lord, heard me. I had hope and love enough to give me limited understanding. Enough to believe that I in fact was not alone. My cry was once again for an explanation. Why the need for all the pain and suffering in the world? For me personally, was my pain necessary for me to be who I am? Was I not a good person at heart? Was there not any good in me at all? Had I not shown others an element of love during my journey here?

Suddenly my cell phone lit up. There were over a dozen messages that came through social media at what appeared to be the same time. Had they been held in a storage cloud above me to be released at this moment? The messages were from people I had not heard from for more than a decade or two. Each individual was letting me know I had been on his or her mind. They expressed they wanted to reach out and let me know what a difference I had made in their lives. The common theme was of the time I had given and the love I had shared with them.

One was from a young man I had not seen for over twenty years. He stated he was not sure if I would remember who he was. He let me know who his parents were. He recalled a time when his parents and he went to dinner with my wife and me. I had graduated from medical school, and my family and I were about to leave for Ohio for my residency training. His parents had been very close friends, and we were taking the time to say goodbye. He was no more than a young child in those days. He said after dinner, outside the restaurant, I had knelt down in front of him. I asked him what his interests were. He replied, "Baseball." I understood that! He said I reached into my pocket and gave him ten dollars. I told him to buy a couple of baseballs and never give up on his dreams. He informed me that he did just that and played baseball for as long as he could. At the time of his message, he said he had been to a park watching his eight-year-old boy play baseball. He said one never knows what a difference is made in another's life in only a moment. I wept.

I got my answer. I had been a decent man. I had given and loved for a long time. Despite my eventual anger and bitterness, which led me into darkness for a time, the light had been and would be forever within me. Pain was part of life. Pain's purpose had been to remind me that the choice was mine: the choice to abide in the light or stumble in darkness. There had been nothing I had or had not done specifically. Pain found me, as it does all of us in this life.

This was a chapter written about change: Changes required to become an accountable adult. Intrinsic change from within created by our desire. External factors played a part in creating choice. Yet each of us chooses to change or not. We know that nothing stays the same in life, so it is reasonable to expect ourselves to internally change so that we may gain peace over the external variations beyond our control. Improvement comes from getting better: Growing from learning. Learning from changing within. Let love guide your internal changes. This ingredient is necessary for a recipe of success. Changes of the heart and soul are what create the everlasting—the everlasting internal cleansing that will create a barrier from uncontrollable external factors.

The choice remains mine and yours to make. What will we do with what has been given? The good, the bad, the ugly. Please remember the difference love can make. Someone else is counting on you, needing your love, more than you are aware. Love continues to be the ultimate resolve for turning pain and anguish into glory.

CHAPTER 4
LESSONS
Accepting imperfection and developing resilience

In the end it's not the years in your life that
count, it's the life in your years.

—Abraham Lincoln

High school was over. Along the way I pumped gas, washed dishes, and bused tables. It was time now to consider my options. One uncle in the family had gone to college, but no others. The family had a background in blue-collar work that included electrical, plumbing, and the railroad. I missed Vietnam by one year. The draft was over the same year I graduated from high school. Some in the family had served during the war. My dad had missed going to war, as I did. One of his brothers, Danny, had cleared jungles in 'Nam, and another uncle, much older, had been an upper turret gunner and flight engineer in a B-24 in World War II. On average, only two planes out of a squadron success-fully completed twenty-five missions. Uncle Shorty's crew completed thirty-five missions. I remember my uncle telling me it was because they flew with God. I heard from his son that he had sat with his dad at a reunion of the flight members. John shared with me that the crew indicated they were alive because of Uncle Shorty. For indeed, Shorty flew with God, and the rest of the crew knew it! He recently passed at the age of ninety. He was a great man. I have a cousin, Tony, who also served in Vietnam. My uncle Herbert served in the army. How I miss Uncle Herb. The time I lived with him and Aunt Lucille I will never forget. How I loved them, and they certainly returned it. I have a nephew who served in more than one of the more recent conflicts. I am certain he dealt with the darkness of war. Chad was awarded a Bronze Star. I recently sat with my cousin Tommy, who was battling colon cancer. We recalled memories and laughed about his father and my mother: how peculiar and mean spirited they both could be. My mother and his father were mirror images of each other. I am proud of Tommy. He revealed no fear knowing death was near. Uncle Robert, Uncle Arvin—more great men. To all my cousins, I love each of you. Special people. Martha, you are a rock! Judy sweet as Aunty Lucille. Solid! Karen and Mary, rest in peace. So you drove a truck for a while, Rod? Heard you took a wrong turn in the road? No worries, cousin. You're not alone. Janet, Faye, Sue, Kevin, David, Jewell, Teresa, Herby Joe, Greg, Vicki, Stacy, Chad, I love you! The song we sang for Tommy's life celebration brought most of us together one more time.

I took a job with a railroad company making tank cars. I also completed a couple of college classes while I pondered. Things were not good at home. There were some good times, as when all the wrestlers came over for a cookout and pool party. (My dad had erected an above-ground pool.) Still, the overwhelming theme was fighting. My brother and I had grown up with it, so in a way it was the norm, though we both knew it was wrong somehow. Going to church didn't stop it, so there was little else to hope for.

It was not as bad as it seemed, however, in that Mother had never been physically hurt up to that time. It had been, more or less, pushing and shoving. Slapping and such. The worst of it was her temper. The verbal attacks. The shouting. The screams that were not really called for. There were rumors of adultery on Mom's part and drinking on Dad's. These accusations were made during arguments. I never knew what was true or false. I only wanted it to end.

The older and stronger I got, the heavier the temptation to intervene became. Yet I refrained. I wondered how much of it had to do with financial strain, but that did not seem to be the case. In those days, people paid cash for everything. Our house was small but furnished well and paid for. Dad always paid cash for his new cars.

I again considered my options, and I decided to invite Mom and Dad down to the local YMCA. I wanted to fix things. I wanted to make things right for people. Looking back through the years, I can now see how it started, this desire to repair what was broken. At times it did not serve me well. That was not the point. I was developing the trait of serving others. I reasoned that in wrestling, I was best on my feet. That's why I shattered the school and state records for takedowns in a dual-meet season. I never liked being on the mat. I never said anything, but the fact was, I was claustrophobic. It had to be psychological: that was why I pinned only a few of my opponents and never got pinned. I liked staying on my feet, just taking other guys down at will and then letting them up. Interesting—there was a form of wrestling in the Olympics referred to as freestyle that favored staying on one's feet. I thought about that but knew even if I competed, there would be a career in coaching when it was over. At the time, my interest wasn't there. There was little way to make a living from wrestling other than coaching or the so-called professional component. This was reserved for physically huge men, and the shows were known to be rehearsed. A form of acting, or so it would seem. Due to my small size and the lack of desire to participate in such rehearsed combat, I considered boxing. So off to the YMCA we went.

My parents didn't know what I was up to, but they went along. When we got there, I asked them to wait while I changed clothes. I had been to the army surplus store and bought a pair of combat boots. I put those on along with shorts, a T-shirt, and sweats—the old-fashioned "Rocky" kind of sweats, not the so-called dries of today. I returned to my folks and asked them to watch. I ran three miles in the boots at eighteen and a half minutes. Not bad, I thought. I then took them into the weight room. After warming up, I bench-pressed 260 pounds. This was over twice my weight; I weighed 125 pounds. I deadlifted 460 pounds off the ground and squatted 360. I never liked the squat. The lift hurt my neck, as the bar seemed to ride too high on me no matter how I tried to adjust. The point is that I was incredibly strong for my size, and fast.

There was a heavy bag hanging. I had bought a pair of boxing gloves. I hit the bag with power and speed as best I could. I had not been trained. Others at the Y stopped and watched. Everyone could hear the cracks and thumps of my hands on the bag as they echoed across the place. My dad looked at me in shock. He and Mom both had been to my wrestling matches, at least most of them. However, it was obvious I was changing, and I could tell my dad was amazed at what he saw.

Then it came: the question. Dad asked, "What is this all about, son?"

I answered, "I was thinking, with your permission I might box for a living. If I could be good enough, maybe you wouldn't have to work anymore, Dad."

I think he really didn't know what to say, but Mom sure did. She slapped me and said, "Are you out of your mind? You could be killed. You will get an education and make something of yourself, like a doctor. What is wrong with you? Let's go home."

The ride home was much like the one from the piano recital. Not much was said. I remember for the first time hating my mother, this woman who had such a tender side and sang at church. She sang to me when I was a child. However, she was cruel in some ways.

Then there was my dad, the man who had told me I would always be small and the only way to keep my lunch money at school was to fight. I remember fighting in the school bathroom on two occasions. I won each of them. I had beaten up bigger boys and somehow knew how to throw punches and even bite if I had to. Soon nobody bothered me. They certainly didn't after the wrestling and weightlifting. Even though I was small, it was obvious the biggest things on my body were my arms and shoulders, so as time passed, boys and men began to look for easier prey. Since I had fought well for free, why not get paid for it?

Sometime later my dad came to me and said, "Son, you don't owe me. No parents want their child hurt."

Little did he know it was too late. They both were killing me; it was just in another way. I never brought up boxing again. I returned to school full time. I wasn't very book smart. I would have to study hard. I did not develop study skills in high school. Too busy wrestling. I thought about returning to wrestling to get a scholarship. They were rare for wrestling in those days. Most went to football and basketball players. It was apparent, though, when I went to a couple of practices, that this would involve all my time. I wasn't gifted enough academically to do what would make Mom happy and wrestle.

In those days medicine was at the top of the food chain. So I entered the ring—the ring of premed. Was it a calling? I suppose, in a way. It wasn't that I didn't like the idea of being a doctor, but anyone reading this can be assured it wasn't fully my idea. Still, it started—my time spent in chasing the white coat and a title. Not a championship belt, but being called *doctor.* I had no idea what responsibility would come with being a physician. For a time, the reality of becoming a physician made me ill, if for no other reason than my inner fear of being inadequate.

Something started in those days that would haunt me forever: the difference between choosing my fate and having it thrust upon me. Thankfully, the day came for me to ask God to help me gain an element of peace about this. And it must have worked, because I remain in medicine to this day. I thank him for the patients I have helped.

Pain had started for me at a young age, and now it was about to take a turn for the worse, a turn that would mark and yet make me. I was only getting started on the journey known as life. Love was distant. The notes were there somewhere, but the melody of sorrow and troubles was the major theme. I was exposed to clinical depression: The dangerous game of physiological changes and emotional imbalance. Needs gone unmet. The vacuum of self-inflicted wounds and the notion of failure, and in this vacuum, searching for mercy and not finding it. Were my thoughts too deep? Did I make it harder than necessary? Was I to be still and know there is a god? That there are reasons for things? Would I have the faith to accept them and not add to the confusion? Perhaps I asked too many questions. It seems I made the worst even more terrifying. Perhaps there is a lot to be said for those who can sit in the silence of unwavering thought and not question the divinity of providence— the why? The why is better left alone.

As I have stated, we never clearly comprehend the reasons for joy and pain. The contentment of not being alone. The agony of learning to be alone after the loss of love, after the solace and peace of believing, even in the darkened silence, that there is someone listening, that being alone is not entirely bad. It is during this time you can finally believe and discover there is a day coming, one in which we will finally be full. We will discover we were never alone. Not really.

I have sat still in the night. I have trembled in fear. Thankfully, at times I gathered enough faith to believe

I am not alone. I ask you to do the same. You will sleep better. Even if you're not able to sleep soundly at times, there can be enough love found in the depths of darkness to quiet the sound of silence. Racing thoughts! Memories! The past! Hope for tomorrow.

Stop! Lie very still. Listen to the stillness. Don't think. Don't think at all. Separate from your mind. Breathe. Breathe in love. Nothing more. Nothing less. Understand you are not alone. You did your best that day. You loved. You chose that. Love is there with you. Why? Because you chose to love, and love remains. Love is lying in the bed with you. You touched another if you loved. And love is caressing you now. It is there. It always has been. Always will be. Let love hold you. Let love close your eyes. Let it allow the sleep and rest you need. Repeat the Lord's Prayer. Use it, my dear friend, my dear precious soul. Let love be all you need. Let love be enough!

CHAPTER 5

LOSS

Rebuilding after a house burns down

There is more wisdom in your body
than in your deepest philosophy.

—*Friedrich Nietzsche*

L ike you, I'm not sure why things happen. I don't
know that many things are intended to be understood. Like a storm that begins to brew and turns into
a hurricane. The result is mass destruction. Why? What
does the powerful form of destruction teach us? Do
we choose to accept the results and petition a higher
power to give us strength to cope rather than find reason to fault and blame a god for allowing such? In the
choice lies our opportunity to create bitterness toward
ourselves and others or love and compassion. All we do

know is that without love, there isn't much left. Not for others as well as ourselves. How do we continue without love?

Some believe all that happens does so for a reason and find a degree of peace in that. Others struggle with free will and what we bring on ourselves. The saint believes in God's will, and the sinner embraces the notion he or she is drowning in it. Perhaps when we draw our last breath and cross over the fence of separation, we can finally balance the equation. Most hope for that, I think. Peace is waiting for those who believe in *love*.

Dad and Mom were falling apart. It was sad and difficult to watch. Dad worked hard. I know he loved Mom. He could have been more romantic at times. Cards and flowers mean a lot. Letting someone know how much he or she is loved. It's very important to do this. Life is short. Those who are fortunate to have decades together and keep the fire burning deep inside are blessed. The old couple who still look and see each other as they did when they first met. Holding hands and holding on. Knowing the painful day will come to say goodbye, yet not wanting to waste a moment. Having the faith that one day they will be together in a better place, where there will be no more sorrow. No more tears. No more goodbyes. Few ever have that, I think. Most long for it. It escapes far too many. I believe it comes down to pride, jealousy, and, quite frankly, selfishness. Not putting the other first. Instead demanding your own desires. Always one taker and one giver—until the giver gives out. Not many have the love only two givers can, that kind of contentment.

Mom was eighteen when she married Dad. She later told me it was to get away from home—not something a mother should say to a son when he has to look at his father. Nor should she have let me know she gave me my middle name because it was the name of the man she really loved. Lord, have mercy! If there had been a time when she had learned to love my father—and I believe she did—it was clear she had forgotten how.

I don't think she was ever really happy or content. Mom was beautiful, and she could sing. I have often wondered, if she had become a famous singer, would her life have turned out different? There was a time when I thought so. Not now. I believe it would have ended the same way.

Mom had an affair. She met a man who was very wealthy. She and Dad separated. My dad was not happy with it, of course. He became very angry and violent. This other man called me to tell me how much he loved my mother. I didn't need to hear that, for I loved both Mom and Dad. We were all on a collision course. This was hard on my brother. I was the oldest and realized he looked for me to somehow deal with it. I was not receptive to my mother's lover when he phoned. How could I be? The affair deteriorated in time. I could go on, but for the sake of the memories of both Mom and Dad and those still alive who might be hurt by knowing, I will make it as brief as I can.

Dad made threats. He was restrained from coming to the house that he had paid for. I guess Mom should have left and gone away with her lover, but she still had two boys at home. The divorce was not final. I was caught in the middle. While trying to work and attend college, I found myself walking the house at night, checking the locks and the windows. I was upstairs one night when it happened. I cannot and will not go into complete detail. Some things are better left private. I will admit my father and mother fought physically, and I joined in. If I hadn't been there, I believe, a life would have been taken.

I struck them both amid the confusion. My brother was there. I regret striking them. The years of torment resulted in a reaction that shocked even me. My brother prevented me from becoming further involved. I was taking it too far. This physical attack from Dad toward Mother had happened one other time. I felt Larry blamed me for not being there. I tried to ensure it wouldn't happen again.

There was violence and emotional damage that went far past the physical bruises. Years of trauma. With the love given, I now understand, there was also severe abuse. Not righteous. Not good. In younger days in Indiana, I could have called my uncle. He had come more than once from down the street and stayed until things were OK. He was a righteous man. I went to see him before he died. We never spoke of these things, but I told him I loved him. He knew why. Uncle Kenneth was a great man.

As we had now relocated back to Tennessee, there was no one to call. It was up to me. I dealt with it in the only way I knew how. It was horrible, and it would stain me for years. I didn't know what else to do, so there we were, standing in the kitchen in the sound of silence. No one could speak. No one could believe what had occurred.

I finally broke the silence. "Mom and Dad, it is over. You will get a divorce and stop."

Dad left. It was hard to believe the decision was mine. Of course, it really wasn't. Mom went to her bedroom. My brother went upstairs. I sat in a chair for what seemed an eternity, angry and wiping away tears. I cried over what I knew would hang with me for life. It has, because I am writing about it now.

Later, Dad called. He apologized to me. He was sincere and told me he loved me. My father never hit me. I regret I cannot say I never hit him. Such things should not happen. They are not the definition of love. They are unfortunate, for they may take years to resolve. Frustration can cause rational thinking to be abandoned. Like a computer that crashes, the mind can only process so much information at once. During these times emotions override one's ability to choose well. As a result, poor choices are made that can take years to resolve. Without the ability to think rationally, we are vulnerable, not only to those who prey upon us but to others who prey upon the vulnerability.

They divorced soon after and sold the house. Larry went away to college for a time. He later joined the military. I stayed to finish school and in time would find myself in the military as well. My dad moved up closer to his job at a nuclear power plant and took refuge and solace on the lake there. However, this would not be the end of the chapter in Tennessee.

In short, my mom became very depressed. There is so much detail but no point in recalling it. I have forgotten some things because I wanted to, but all that matters, really, is the result of the madness. My mom became so ill that she made several suicide attempts. I had her admitted to a psych hospital. Going to visit her, seeing her in restraints, hearing her screaming at me to get her out was more than I could bear. The irony is I went to my dad for help. He still loved her. Her so-called lover had long since disappeared.

Dad came back and bought another home. We all moved in and tried to help Mom, but to no avail. I left her alone one day a little too long. Despite all the efforts and aborted attempts, she finally got the job done. Mom took her life. Dad found her when he came home from work.

It was as if I knew when it happened. I had been with her but left briefly to see a friend and get some groceries. Before I left she kissed me and told me I was a good son. She seemed fine. Later I realized it had only been an act. I don't think how she said it hit me until I was shopping at the store. I felt a sense of panic and, leaving the cart, ran to a phone and called home. There was no answer. I phoned a neighbor, who informed me an ambulance had been to the house and left. I drove immediately to the local hospital.

I met my dad and brother in the ER. Dad had found Mom when he came home from work. My brother was back and forth from school. This was before his years in the military. It's painful to recall, so my timeline could be a little off. I do remember seeing my dad from across the ER and him shaking his head. Larry and I went in to see Mom, her blue face and cold body on a gurney. We both told her we were sorry and we loved her. What else could we say? Our mom was gone. The utter despair felt like a weight I couldn't bear. The preacher who spoke at my mom's funeral referred to her as a "fine diamond" that "never got a chance to shine."

It was more than difficult choosing a coffin. Her past requests haunted me. I made sure she was buried in the dress she had chosen with me in the privacy of her bedroom only a month earlier. Of course, I had hoped this wouldn't happen. I recall believing that was the worst thing that would ever happen to me in this life. I was young. I lived on and experienced worse.

Dad sold the second house after we buried Mom. He returned to the lake. All our relationships were strained.

I worked for the railroad a short time before the military. My dad's younger brother helped me get the job. He was an engineer. At one time my grandfather on my dad's side of the family had been a conductor. The family had a strong connection to the railroad. Many of my great uncles also had a railroad background. They collectively ran a small station for a while. I rode the train as a child and to this day enjoy walking through the historical train station here in Kansas City.

I lost the job when it was stated during a work physical that I had scoliosis—a curvature of the spine. I was misdiagnosed. I never actually had it, not now or then. Another life-changing event. The reasoning for their letting me go? At the time, the railroad was dealing with disabilities and legal matters relating to back conditions—injuries and so forth—claimed by many of their hired personnel. They therefore targeted anyone without years of employment and who was considered an unnecessary risk.

Another turn in the road. Would I have stayed? As I stated, the military finally found both my brother and me. I sold my car before I left and bought my brother a motorcycle, which he had for some time. It was an effort to let him know I was sorry about everything.

I've thought about this event a lot through the years. I wondered how it might have been different. Yet it was no different in the end for Elvis and countless others. At some point Mom lost her joy and peace. Even her faith in

God had escaped her. No doubt she had severe depression. Of course, there was intense shame and guilt for what she had done. For some, life becomes too much to bear. Like a punch-drunk fighter taking one too many blows. These are the things that frame us. The pain that develops us. The great equalizer. It is said Christ suffered on the cross. This life can be at times the cross we also bear. It becomes a choice. How do we deal with it? Will it make us stronger? Will we surrender to the same fate as my mom? God tells us to give the cross to him! We simply cannot bear the weight on our own.

I can say I chose at that time in my life never to ever lay hands on my wife with anger should I marry. Also never to be unfaithful. Never to expose my kids to such. I made a choice. These thoughts and many more came to me through the death of a would-be angel.

My dad and I healed over time. He remarried Odie, his high school sweetheart. My relationship with him grew strong and was filled with love in his last twenty years, in part due to my stepmom—not only her love, but the love of her children. Cheryl and Anita, I love you. Bud and Van. George and Deloris. Thank God for her and the love she gave us all. She knows I love her very much. I will forever be grateful to her for loving my dad. Thank you, Odie. My God, the love her daughters have shown in caring for her in her older years!

I understood something during that time that had never occurred to me before. My dad must have resented me. In many ways my mom showed me more love than she did him. At least she confided in me more. It wasn't my fault, but it was true nonetheless. Thank God Dad and I overcame that, and our love held up for his later decades. I found the love of my dad again, and he found mine. I know my dad was a good man. I think for him, the partnership with my mother was simply toxic. As hard as it might be, there are times in our lives when the best choices are simple, no matter how difficult we make them. It is hard to surrender and walk away from love that is one sided.

In the latter part of Dad's life, he developed Parkinson's. His battle with that disease lasted about two years. When Dad died my brother didn't appear to forgive him for the years of difficulties with mom. He blamed me for his not knowing of Dad's passing. I think, given that I had informed him of Dad's illness, his choices were his to make. I believed I had made too many for him in the past, and he resented me for doing so. I was in a no-win situation. He did not attend the funeral, and my son, my brother's son, my dad's brothers, and I carried the casket. My uncles stood by me and held me up. They were and are great men.

Sadly, my brother and I have not spoken since our father died—something else that was and is our collective choice. It does hurt. He is my brother. I do love him. I simply don't see what I did to him that was wrong. He once told me he was Cain and I was Abel. I know how that story went. It seemed safer for us both to walk away. I had seen what happened when people didn't.

I attended a conference once where the speaker recommended spending time with those who forgive and return love given, and leaving others alone. Made sense to me. My brother has his own version, I am certain. Not long ago I reached out to him on Facebook. I'm not too good on the internet, so it is possible he didn't get it. I don't hate my brother. I can't say if he hates me. At least for a time, it seemed so. I remain hopeful that he finds peace, and he may have already. All I can do at this time is love him from a distance and believe that for whatever he perceived or believed I failed in, I am forgiven. I have forgiven him for the same. Perhaps life can simply create enough confusion that we get lost in the whirlwind. I do know it was never my intent to hurt him. For things I did wrong, brother, I am sorry.

There have been ministers cruel enough to tell me my mother is in hell. I maintain that is only fear on their part. Regardless, I do not choose to believe it. I believe her soul rests along with many others that were restless here. That is my choice. She definitely lived in hell here, most of it self-inflicted. She was mentally ill. I have learned pain can be cruel, yet mercy is greater. I believe some can find no moral solution for their agony. It is possible to believe the only hope for peace is to find it in another life.

I have treated many patients with physical pain. Most of them have experienced emotional pain as well.

Sometimes psychiatric issues need to be treated as much as or more than the physical pain. It is sad that all one hears about is abuse and addiction. Not much attention is given to those who have benefited from appropriate pain management that resulted in a higher level of functioning. The pendulum never rests in the middle; it's always swinging from one side to the other. My empathy toward legitimate suffering remains. Again, as in many things, the few manage to ruin much for the many.

People are people no matter what they do. Society tends to elevate some above anything realistic. Actors. Athletes. Those with money. How many of those lives end in tragedy? Were they unable to live up to the expectations of others, or was it that inside they chased demons of their own? I have heard nationally renowned speakers indicate that almost everyone has something he or she needs help with. Dark secrets. The ghosts that haunt in the middle of the day as well as in the empty night. I recall during my youth the idea of love in any form was only that: an idea. Not reality, just a foolish notion. I learned fear more than anything. No doubt fear can erase productivity and is a negative that consumes great amounts of energy.

Mom didn't live life on her terms. Life was what happened while she existed. It happened to her and not for her. At times I have repeated the same theme. I can credit myself for making the effort to live differently. I give myself that. There are times when our best is good enough and other times when our best is pathetic and falls so horribly short. Our best on a Monday just isn't the same as it is on a Friday. The difference? Fatigue!

I apologize, Mom. My best failed you. I have to say, though, was it fair of you to ask me to understand your insanity? Is it not true that you also failed me? Can we give each other the grace to forgive and rest with knowing neither of us set out to hurt the other? This is a powerful form of love. I can say this about loss: it will force you to count the cost, to call insanity into reason and, in doing so, gain some understanding and strength for other losses to come. One of the hardest things to do in a situation of traumatic despair and turmoil is not to let guilt engulf you. At some point one has to let go of guilt, or the ability to reason will never come.

I am confident each of you recalls your first great loss: The pain that dwelled within it. The possible inability to ever let it go. The steady walk again, only when you have made the choice to live with it better than the day before. I ask you to remember once again that in the still of the night, you are not alone, despite what faith or the lack of it affords you, regardless of your beliefs. Know this: Others have felt your pain. I have experienced your brokenness. I am another traveler like you. My skin color may not be the same as yours. We may have other differences. My blood runs red, though. Like yours.

Pain is inevitable in this life. Shame and guilt are products of fear. Better that we live as instructed and not be afraid. Pain will be served. Grief will follow at some point and in one form or another. Those who learn and practice the joy of living beyond the confinement of pain are blessed for doing so. If you are tired of living, it's quite possible life has beaten you severely and pain has taken its toll. The truth is you are not alone. It is not easy to take continual beatings in life. To say so is indeed a lie. Love can ease it. If you choose to keep loving, to freely give love despite how deep your sorrow may be, you will find the grip of pain loosens. Love will allow you to let it go enough to live again. I have found it to be the only available method for dealing with life's pain.

My God, I hope someone reads this, if for no other reason than to hear this: I love you. I am tired, at times very fatigued. Love encourages me to continue on. My pain is nothing compared to what some of my patients have endured. Countless times I have walked out of a treatment room and retreated to whatever empty space I could find. Once there I asked for forgiveness, for complaining about my issues. I have been amazed more than once that some of these patients continued to live on! However, it is our instinct to survive.

It has been my choice to share my story. You have yours. I have mine. The only thing I believe that matters is that each of us realize—realize that without love, we have no story at all. Not one that matters.

I believe that man will not merely endure:
he will prevail. He is immortal, not because
he alone among creatures has an inexhaust-
ible voice, but because he has a soul, a spirit
capable of compassion and sacrifice and
endurance. The poet's, the writer's, duty is to
write about these things.

A man is the sum of his misfortunes. One day
you'd think misfortune would get tired, but
then time is your misfortune.

—William Faulkner

Grief never ends
But it changes
It's a passage
Not a place to stay
Grief is not a sign of weakness
Nor a lack of faith
Grief is the price of love

—Author Unknown

CHAPTER 6

DISCIPLINE
Letting the fire of regret burn out

Now life is the only art that we are required
to practice without preparation, and with-
out being allowed the preliminary trials, the
failures and botches, that are essential for the
training of a mere beginner.

—*Lewis Mumford*

Joining the military was one of the best things I ever
did. Of course, there were games played in basic
training. Those stories are well known to anyone who
has served. I will detail an example later in the chapter.
I found solace in being a part of something bigger than
myself. It felt good to serve and to wear my country's

uniform. I think the respect demanded and given was part of the appeal. After all, it was the opposite of my home life, so why wouldn't it make sense?

Though I had graduated college, I enlisted as an airman first class. I was glad I did, for it gave me a perspective I would not have known and more respect from others in the military. What made my experience a little different from some was that I started in the air force but ended up in the army. I completed less than two years of active duty and another six or so in the reserve. I never believed I would go to medical school, as it was something at least in part my mom had chosen. Regardless, the idea returned after her death, perhaps in association with the guilt I felt over her suicide. It was a method of becoming a commissioned officer. I was released from active duty and placed in the reserve to attend medical school.

There were no air force units near the medical school. I was transferred to the army and commissioned as an officer. The military did not pay for medical school, however, due to the economy at the time. The military had more applications than scholarships available. This resulted in many deserving applicants being turned down for the financial assistance. Some who received funding certainly shouldn't have, if for no other reason than they didn't appreciate the scholarship and had no intention of serving as a physician in the military any longer than they had to. I went so far as to visit with a high-ranking officer who served on the scholarship selection committee. He readily admitted the process of selection was poor, as were the results. Over time the process was improved.

Once I completed med school, I achieved the rank of captain in the reserve. During my residency in anesthesia, my time in the military ended, but the choice was not only mine; it also rested with my spouse and the obligation of raising three children. I explained to my wife that I was offered major for a day to satisfy the need not to skip a rank, and then lieutenant colonel to reenlist. Not a bad opportunity for a thirty-four-year-old. The medical corps is not like the rest of the military. I would never be leading troops into battle. I didn't need to be a West Point graduate to provide medical care. This was a reserve offer. I could have gone back into active military with the same rank offered.

My military record was outstanding in every way. I could have easily exceeded the rank offered—unless I irritated the wrong general. Still, my school debts were heavy, and the pay was not as high as civilian medical practice. There was the chance I would be called to deploy in case of a conflict or war. For these reasons the mother of my children was against my taking the offer. I was honorably discharged.

As it turned out, the medical detachment I had been part of was made active no more than forty days after my discharge. They were all on their way to Desert

Storm. I had taken the civilian road in the service and had donned the uniform of a spouse and father. As I have been reminded many times, one cannot be in two places at once. My heart goes out to those who were taken away from their families and, of course, especially to those who never returned. I have listened to others who now serve in Congress or as TV commentators who have served against their families' wishes. I have thought about that many times. Like them, I made a choice. If there is a universal truth, it is that life demands sacrifice in so many ways.

I can say I miss the uniform. I miss the respect given and returned. Of course, my perspective was not that of someone who witnessed the horror of war. The highest compliment I've ever been given as a doctor was the .45-caliber handgun one of my patients carried while serving on a riverboat in Vietnam. He said the weapon, which had taken life, would be better served being held by someone who had spent decades trying to do the opposite as well as reduce the pain of those suffering. Anything and all I ever contributed to the military could not measure up to this gift—a gift made to a man who had chosen to take the uniform off by a soldier who kept it on and knew the pain of war. What an honor it was to serve and treat him.

I never had to face war. Timing never seemed to be a friend of mine, but in this regard, it was. I missed two conflicts by a narrow margin.

I previously mentioned basic training. On my first day, the bus pulled up, the drill sergeants got on, and we got off with their help. Standing in line side by side, with luggage at our feet, we were from everywhere, with nothing yet everything in common. We lost our identities along with our hair and any individuality at all.

The barracks, with the long line of beds, became home. We emptied the luggage we had and replaced it with green canvas bags. What came out of those suitcases we had brought and mistakenly thought we could keep changed my role at the onset. Out of my case fell a pair of jeans and a shirt or two, as well as boxing gloves and a college diploma. When the drill sergeant saw that, the questions came.

"You graduate from college?"

I said, "Yes."

He was confused. "What are you doing enlisted?"

I indicated that officer training school had not expressed interest in my biology degree. I wasn't sure I wanted to go to medical school. Jobs were hard to find, so I had enlisted.

"You box?"

"Not really," I replied.

"Can you fight or not?"

"I can."

He replied, "You are dorm chief."

I asked him what that meant.

He said, "You'll find out. Now shut up."

I soon came to realize that being dorm chief meant anytime he was not around, I was in charge. He would blame me for anything that went wrong. Keeping the barracks clean—toilets, beds, lockers. Marching. I got involved up to my ass in all of it. I soon realized that trying to force fifty guys I didn't know to do what they didn't want to do was unpleasant at best. I tried to quit the position, which went over like a turd on the floor with the sergeant. He told me to either get it together or get ready to repeat boot camp. That I didn't want!

So I got real, which means unreal and unrighteous. I got mean as hell and turned over more than one bunk. I was tough for my size and never bluffed. There is always one, though. He was big and strong. Antonio didn't want to comply with the rules of the day, and soon mutiny started. The day came when I had no choice. It was Antonio or me. I had been in a few fights and won them all. I had beaten a young man half to death outside a shopping mall when he tried to run over a crowd including me as we left a movie theater. He was larger, but I was very quick and strong. Besides, I had just buried my mom and wasn't in a good frame of mind. I had a year between college and the military when I struggled emotionally. I thank God I didn't get into more trouble than I did.

I squared off with Antonio in the latrine. He stated he would beat the hell out of me. I said he would know I was there, for I would not be defeated easily, and if I lost, he had to sleep sometime. In other words, I would have revenge if necessary. He didn't like that. At that moment it occurred to him I might be crazy. I informed him he was correct. We formed a truce that day.

I never had any more trouble being dorm chief. If anyone was out of line, all I had to do was have Antonio take care of it. We ended up first in our section in dorm cleanliness and second in marching.

The end of basic training came, and I was asked to stay on and become a drill sergeant. I declined and moved on to the US Air Force School of Aerospace Medicine, where I helped with research. I say I helped, but I was a test subject more than anything. I tried out everything from liquid cooling garments being tested for airstrip repairs in the desert in case of chemical warfare to hyper- or hypo-pressurized chambers. From there I reconnected with the idea of returning to medical school. The time I spent as an enlisted man, with three square meals a day, was like sitting on the stool between rounds. It was a much-needed pause that helped me heal from pain, to prepare for more of life and what it would bring.

In the end it was not my destiny to stay in the military. The woman who demanded I leave passed away and left me to raise three young children on my own. Again fate dealt its cruelty. How could I have served while also being a single parent of eight-, ten-, and twelve-year-olds. Even though you could not have known, Tamara, dear wife and mother, thank you for making the choice for me to leave the military. I doubt it would have made parenting any simpler.

Sometimes we doubt our choices and wonder what would have happened if we had turned left rather than right. I might be retired today had things gone differently. My wife had the instinct to let her mind apply reason. In the end she did what mothers should do: she protected her children. My uniform and duty were chosen for me. I wore the ribbons of a father and a mother and bore the battle scars that would come with the responsibilities. No pension came from the sacrifice I made. It is what it is.

I was proud to serve my country and thank God for the discipline I learned in the process. To the drill sergeants, soldiers, medical providers, and countless others, thank you for all you've done. Understanding the regimen of the soldier has helped me relate to others who have served. I have always believed that those who serve deserve honor. One can only hope that those who have endured losses of limbs or lives for our country experience peace in the next life. Those who are gone are missed.

If today's youth could experience the discipline of the military without the madness or hell of war, I would advise enlisting. Since one is not guaranteed without the possibility of the other, it can be a hard choice to make. My son asked me about being a US Navy SEAL. I discouraged it. I was a physician in the military with the mission of saving lives. I was uncertain of the choice to be trained to take lives. I had treated and been exposed to many veterans who saw and engaged in combat and suffered with PTSD. As is also well known, many of these veterans have committed suicide after returning home. Knowing these things gave me pause regarding my son. In looking back upon the trouble that found him regardless, I gave further consideration to his idea. Would that have saved him from poor choices that caused trouble? Would it have resulted in an honorable death or coming home without the use of his limbs? Regardless I did ask myself if I repeated the action of my mother decades before by influencing the choices of my son.

My daughter told me once, "Dad, you have regrets about things based on your belief that taking another path would have turned out better. The truth is you do not know what you or we might have been saved from. You did your best. Try to have peace." Good advice. I am now confident that others who understand the hell of war would tell me I enjoyed the military because I did not experience war. War is hell. I have no doubt this is true.

Recently I visited with a patient who had lost his son in the current wars. The pain on his face was noticeable. He expressed that he had talked his son into serving in the military. His son had been killed in Iraq. Thankfully, while I was visiting with my son, he told me to have peace, for he said he had gained peace in not serving. That was enough for me. The troubles and violence he expressed might have resulted in medals of valor during war. These actions could also have resulted in his returning home in a body bag, or perhaps in a condition considered worse than death.

How can any of us know what is best? The view when looking back, with the knowledge of how things turned out, is clear. All we have when we make choices is the perspective at the time. It is a common theme that the twenty-twenty vision in the rearview mirror haunts us. The regret. The disturbing hell that leads to restless nights of insomnia. The mirror is there for a reason: to help us learn and change. To be smarter. Careful. Still, if all we do is ponder ourselves into paralyzing regret, we can no longer move at all, so it's far better to remove the mirror and look rather into the larger car windshield in front of us.

I do have regrets, those imposed by others creating a secondary response. Therefore, we blame ourselves for things we truly didn't own. This creates confusion. Then there is regret created by our own choices. Either way it is best to choose not to live in the continuum of regret. Some regret can be permanent. For example, once a limb is lost, you will not get it back. People who learn to embrace regret, however, move into acceptance. In doing so they can love again. They choose not to live in regret because to do that would be like falling in love with it, continually mourning for what could have been. We all have our book of regrets. The embrace allows us to close the book and write another chapter. The acceptance encourages us to live ahead of regret. Living and loving life in regret is a disservice to God and family. Regret can actually become an addiction. For one to dance again, regret is accepted and embraced. This allows us not to be paralyzed by it. Regret prevents freedom. Within this prison it is rather impossible to receive or give love. As in the Sinatra song "My Way," regrets are admitted to being there but are too few to mention. I think what this means is we have embraced the regrets to the extent they are not worth mentioning. We in fact own regret. It does not own us. In doing it "our way," with the warm embrace of regret, we in fact transform it into love. Every wrong creates an opportunity for right. Every door that closes offers an open window and another means of moving on.

Dance when you can. Most find dancing relaxing and fun. To keep in step, there is no time for idle thoughts, no time to be afraid. Do you remember how to dance? Did you ever try? It is not too late. It will take courage. Energy. If we get up and make the effort, the dance can free us from the blame and shame of regret. How beautiful to see those whose youth have passed them by, yet with wrinkled smiles and tapping feet, they dance! I believe this is because they have successfully managed regret by embracing it and transforming it into everlasting acceptance and love.

CHAPTER 7

RINGS

Fighting the good fight

You cannot be disciplined in great things and
undisciplined in small things.
If a man does his best, what else is there?
Success is how high you bounce when you hit
the bottom.
Courage is fear holding on a minute longer.

—General George Patton

I guess it would be somewhat natural that after a decade, I would return to the time I had invited my folks to the YMCA. The circle of life finds its way back to a starting point. While I was a resident giving anesthesia for trauma and obstetrics, a classmate invited me to attend a Golden Gloves boxing tournament. There was no shortage of fighters in the Youngstown, Ohio, area, as Don King's camp was not far. Many amateurs and professionals had started their careers there. I sat there, popcorn and Coke in my lap, and said to my friend, "I always thought I could have done that."

He looked at me like he needed to call a code and to defibrillate me. He said, "Are you nuts?"

Of course I knew I was and had been for a while. He didn't. My wife did. So when I went home and asked what she thought about me seeing if I could prove I could win the Golden Gloves, she indicated that for the first time she was sure of it: she had wed an insane man. It was something I had heard before from another woman in my life, as I have shared regarding the YMCA with Mom and Dad. This time I was not going to let it go. The mind, trying to restrain the heart with all its logic, just couldn't win the fight. I had to know. To this day I don't really understand why, but maybe it was to prove something to myself, or to show something to a parent who had not believed in me, or at the least to allow me to choose my own fate. No matter. I simply knew I had to see if I could do it.

I had to ask my residency trainer if it would be OK. He was an amazing man. He had been a wrestling champ in high school, so we already had common ground, but he had to think this one over. After all I had a job to do at the hospital, and any boxing training I did could not interfere with that. Like me, I don't think he had any idea where we were headed. But for some reason, he agreed. Maybe he reasoned, as my wife and others did, that after I got the crap beat out of me, it would be over. They were both right and wrong.

I found out where a nearby gym was and walked in. After the trainer heard my request, he told me I had to be out of my mind. But within minutes I had headgear on and was in the ring with last year's Golden Gloves champion. Although he was near my weight, he was ten years younger and on the cusp of turning pro. He kicked the shit out of me in moments. With my head tilted back and a towel to my nose, I thought if I could stop the flow of blood, and if my eye didn't turn black and blue, maybe it wouldn't be so bad.

The trainer must have thought, *Lesson learned. Maybe this fool can get himself home. And that will be the end of that.* I did find my way home. I didn't know how to avoid my wife, so I just faced her.

"My God, what have you done?" she asked.

What could I say? I had my ass kicked. I loved Tamara and always will. She had every right to be upset.

Even my son was a little shocked, asking, "What happened, Daddy?"

Words failed me. I finally came up with "Daddy fell down." Well...I had. I'd just had some help.

The next day my residency trainer realized what he had said yes to. Joe was like, "Lynn, really?" Of course, there was nothing for me to do but see patients looking as if I had been in a bar fight. God bless Joe. He let it go.

So, then, what was I going to do? Quit fighting, right? Nope! Too much pride. Too much ego. I have learned as I have aged that these traits are not good ones and will usually lead me to trouble. I don't claim to be full of wisdom, but let me say this: I had less of it back then.

I returned to the gym after I had healed up a little. The trainer was not amused this time. He put me back in with the champion (who, I think, felt a little bit sorry for me). He was black, and I'm white. I'm not stereotyping when I say most blacks in boxing at that time were strong and fast. I don't know if I did any better this time, but he didn't beat me up as badly. I even hit him a few times. I did well enough to decide to stick with it.

I trained hard, but what can one do in a month? Next thing I knew, I was on a fight card for an out-of-town bout. To this day I thank God for that. The fight was put on by the Hells Angels in Erie, Pennsylvania. Like an idiot, I went. I will never forget my opponent, Johnny Cave Man. He beat me from head to toe. I survived and got in a couple of licks that at least got his attention, but I didn't win. For the most part, he beat the hell out of me.

After that first fight, things turned around. I fought a local fight, still not realizing that amateur fights are not scored like professional fights. Trying to knock someone out and hitting him with heavier blows does not count any more than a crisp combination. Despite the first loss and another, I gained the attention of two men. They were angels sent from God who felt bad for the local doctor who was trying to become a boxer. I guess it was their mission in life to save mine. After we talked and I joined this father-and-son duo, they taught me the art and science of boxing. We put together a garage gym. They also had been out of the game for a while. The father, Ted, had been an amateur champion, and the son, Terry, was an ex-professional.

Training intensified, and step by step I learned how to execute a perfect right cross. They said there wasn't time enough to concentrate on a left hook, but they felt if I was in better condition than my opponent and could deliver the jab and right with power, I would win. They told me they had never seen anyone my weight with such power, and that gave me a lot of much-needed confidence.

The night of the fight, several medical providers from the hospital showed up—either because they knew I was due for a win or because they felt they could give me CPR if all else failed. But I won my first fight! It was hell, and my opponent nearly took my head off, but I won. He was as tough as any I had faced. I hurt him, though. I never understood how, after I had turned his head so hard with a right hook that echoed across the venue, he stayed upright. He did, though. We exchanged toe to toe until the final bell.

It seemed to me that my opponents were not getting any weaker. Was I handling them better? It had been almost a year since I had popped off to my colleague that I wanted to fight in the Golden Gloves, and here I was in the ring. Terry and Ted were happy with my progress. Even my wife was beginning to believe I might live through this.

I have to give further credit where it is due. During this time, I had my own doubts. I called my father-in-law, who treated me like the son he never had until the damage between my father and me had healed. What a beautiful man. To this day my love for him escapes words. I asked him, "Dad, should I go through with this? I think the opponents may be worse than those at the beginning."

He replied, "Son, there is one life. Go for it!"

That was all I needed to hear. I love my father-in-law and mother-in-law.

I made it to the finals. I weighed in at 126 and was in the best shape of my life. As I recall, no one showed for 126. I was not going to go home without a fight after all my hard work, so I moved up to fight an opponent at 132. I didn't fight in the open division which is reserved for those with too many fights to remain novice, but rather because I was too old to fight as a novice. If I won and kept winning, I would fight at the nationals. Winning also qualified one for the Olympic trials, though at that point no one was looking for that.

My residency trainer had already told me the hospital administration had enough of my coming in and treating patients with black eyes and such. Of course the mother of my kids had withstood more than enough. The point is this was it for me. Either fight or be a physician. How ironic! Win or lose, this would be it. It would have been hard to compete at a national level anyway, with the opponents getting tougher and having even more experience. I can't imagine I would have advanced very far.

The opponent that evening must have thought, My God! He's going up in weight and shouldn't even be in the open. He's had fewer than six fights and is thirty-two years old. I will defeat him with ease. I wouldn't have blamed him. For some reason, though, I had no fear. I knew what I could do now. I knew my strength and my speed. I knew how I had trained. Ted and Terry were there, and my wife was bringing our little son. I think even she believed I had a chance. My middle daughter was too young to attend, and the youngest was still in her mother's tummy.

Unless my opponent took my life, I was determined to beat him. I recalled what my father-in-law had said, and I was not going home without that trophy. This was for all the fights I'd never gotten to have. This was for all the piano lessons. This was for the college graduation my mother didn't attend. This was for the doctor I had become when I didn't even know whether it was my dream or moms. This was for it all.

Ted and Terry found me at the hot dog stand eating when it was time. I didn't even hear the call to report to the ring. As I entered the ring and took off my robe, I was a cut and trim 126 pounds (plus a hot dog). I was ready. After all, what else could happen? I had already been beaten up. My life up to then had already offered more trauma than this.

The truth is I had underestimated my opponent, but not as much as he had me. He had no neck, so rotating his head was impossible. He was a southpaw. I had no idea how to fight someone from the left. I found out by missing him with my right while he nearly took off my head with his left. I remember thinking, *How can this be happening? I am ready. He is no tougher than me…or is he? What the hell is going on?*

I was throwing jabs, but I was missing. I followed with a right that should have sent him to the canvas; instead, I kept missing. He countered with a left that nearly caused me to collapse. Some of the medical staff from the hospital attented. The place held about two thousand people. This could not be happening.

Thank almighty God, the bell rang. I went to my corner and asked Ted and Terry, "What is going on?" If they hadn't been there, my opponent would have dropped me in round two. They told me he was a southpaw, so I had to reverse everything. Move to my left and not my right. Wait for him to throw a punch, let him miss, and then counter with my right. After I tagged him and he felt my power, I would go to the body and don't hold anything back. Let him feel my power.

I went back for round two and did what they said. I moved in the opposite direction. He threw and missed, and I didn't react. I was shaken and not confident. I waited. He threw again and missed. I still waited. Then, above all the other voices in the crowd of two thousand, I heard one voice: "Daddy!" It was my son.

I couldn't wait again. It was now or never. My opponent threw and missed. I threw my punch and nailed him with a right from hell. He buckled. He was too tough to go down with that, but the blow registered. I attacked. I went to the body and took his feet two inches off the canvas. I jabbed and this time hit him with three blows in a row. Another right and then back to the body. The tide had turned. He was hurt. I knew it, and so did he. The bell rang. We had one round each now. It would be the third and final round that mattered.

I was not tired at all. He was. Ted and Terry wanted me to finish him, and I should have. But I couldn't do it. It was too late. I had been trained as a doctor to help and save. All I wanted to do was to win.

My opponent would never believe this. I would not expect him to. I let him go. He was satisfied to tie me up for the third round. I knew I could break free and knock him out. Still, I couldn't do it. He didn't deserve it, in my opinion. How could anyone be a boxer extending mercy like that? It was proof to me that my time was gone. I was a doctor, not a fighter. I just didn't want to hurt him anymore. I figured I had done enough to win. Looking back, I realize it could have resulted in a loss.

I took the split decision and won the Golden Gloves. Not by the margin it could have been, but it was a grateful win for me. With the attitude I had, I easily could have lost. I felt bad for my opponent. I knew what it was like to lose. In other words, my days back at the YMCA were forever gone. I had made my choice and would never be able to do harm to anyone again unless someone was trying to hurt me or my family. You can't win in boxing if you don't have the killer's instinct. One of my patients told me years later that Joe Frazier's trainer, Yank Durham, once told her this about her boyfriend and his fighter, Len Hutchins. He went on to become the number-one-ranked light heavyweight in the world, but he didn't have the killer's instinct.

Life is so strange. An element of time and place. What could have been and what might have? I went on to train a club of troubled young men and had several champions. One considered a professional career. My son also became a champion. But always fighting was not the primary goal; it was about life and how you play the game.

I tried to teach the boys for the short time I had them the same thing I had learned from my brief fighting career. Boxing is like life: unfair and corrupted by greed. Sometimes we get hit below the belt. At times the decision will be wrong. Who really wins, even though we all put in the hard and honest work? In the end all that matters is that you go out swinging. You give it your best.

I was once told I might be the only doctor who ever won a Golden Gloves title. I did see years ago a physician from another country who was here fighting professionally. I guess he never got a title shot, or he quit, because I never heard much about him. Of course, none of that really matters. It could be said that most physicians would not be in the type of physical shape to be boxers or that they are much too smart to try. Since physicians have performed and done well in many other sports, it may be the latter.

What I can say is during my fight, I heard the bell sound and responded. Isn't that what each of us should do? Answer the bell? Looking back, I can see that although I had been blinded by hatred, love was there. It remained, and I was giving it. Do we play to win? I suppose so. In the end, however, I think it is our growth in trying that truly allows us to contribute greatness in this life. It is far greater to endure the blows and get up than to run away.

I recently reviewed some accounts of the disaster of September 11, 2001. Without question those who risked their lives to save others, even when it appeared they would certainly die, were living on a different level than those who thought only of their own right to live. So many are now tormented by the memory of choosing themselves to the point they are saddened by taking another breath. No one blames them, for some had families to consider. It was interesting, though, to see the reactions of these survivors. It was as if they felt cheated—cheated that they had not chosen death with honor rather than life with self-imposed disgrace. One thing is evident: there are people in this world who are not all about themselves. Thank the universe for that!

It has been sad to witness the recent years of terrorism. So much innocent life taken in the name of a god that will reward those who have chosen to participate in this insanity. The view is that somehow our country is to blame; all the while, tens of thousands flee from oppression to get here. To America. To the outstretched arms that offer refuge and hope for better lives. Or, at the least, once did.

Now this new war has us confused. We know not who the enemy is or where he is hiding or even what he stands for. The more painful truth is that the enemy will not compromise. Is this religion? Is anyone from any faith protected outside of those who would appear insane? They will not accept love. The only resolve is ordering our own to find and kill them, only to be reminded not to ponder why. Is there a god that is watching? Asking others to once again have faith no matter the lack of understanding? Faith that a better place awaits? That offers eternal love? The same paradise that others who are taking life in the name of God choose to believe in? What kind of god would that be? What chance would any of us have?

In the process many have lost trust in our own leaders. Politics has become an endless pit of corruption and greed. There is no offer of compromise, only paralyzing gridlock!

There cannot be love in murder. If we are to hang on to anything of substance and truth, let us do this:

hang on to love. We must do what we have to do. In the midst of callous hatred, I pray you and I hang on. Cling to a higher purpose. Even in the face of the death of another, offer love despite the need for painful resolve. Love remains the only common thread of decency we have. Even if this must be tough love, its purpose is to stop the loss of innocent life. At its end, despite the damage this kind of hatred can create, let each of us not forget how to love.

If this seems awkward and difficult to accept, do this: ask yourself how you define love. What does it mean? What is its purpose? I am confident we all ponder this from time to time. I have made a mess of things. I never saw it coming. Thank God for love. It is all I have left. Funny, isn't it? It was all that ever mattered.

We understand that in and of ourselves we are not love. We can only aspire to be love.

> *Love is patient, love is kind. It does not envy,*
> *it does no boast, it is not proud. It does not*
> *dishonor others, it is not easily angered, it*
> *keeps no record of wrongs. Love does not*
> *delight in evil but rejoices with the truth. It*
> *always protects, always trusts, always hopes,*
> *always perseveres.*

—*1 Corinthians 13*

CHAPTER 8

MEDICINE
Eternity offers the final cure

*Mankind must put an end to war before war
puts an end to mankind.*

—*John F. Kennedy*

*Let me assert my firm belief that the only thing
we have to fear is fear itself—nameless, unrea-
soning, unjustified terror which paralyzes
needed efforts to convert retreat into advance.*

—*Franklin D. Roosevelt*

One of the most difficult and painful things I have
endured is the practice of medicine, even though
it is considered a noble cause. I think in part the pain

for me was due to the belief it was something my mom wanted more than I did. Ironically, in many ways it has been rewarding.

When I applied to medical school, admission was very competitive. Doctors were well respected and were paid better than people in most other professions. There still are a few specialties where cash payment dominates. Those doctors often earn more than most physicians. Somewhere along the way came the perception that doctors are overpaid. No one focuses on the cost of pharmacology or technical advances. To most people it seems the answer is to control the physician's pay, and all problems with the cost of medical care will be resolved. No one ever thinks about the years we spent in training, earning very little, working seventy to eighty hours a week while piling up massive debt from school loans. There are current studies that reveal physicians many times are closing in on forty years of age before school debts are retired and income is realized. The hard truth is there are many who do better, all things considered. All I can say is that medical care and insurance coverage remain difficult for most people to obtain. Obviously, there are other factors involved in cost control.

I cannot understand war. Why? I have never been to war. I have been told what it was like. It is madness. *Madness!* I can never understand childbirth for obvious reasons. The point is there are some things each of us has experienced that are not explainable to others who have not. For those of you who are not physicians, I cannot explain what it is like to be one. What I can say is the difficulty in receiving appropriate medical care is not entirely the fault of the physician.

Then what is it about the practice of medicine that makes it rewarding, despite the failed financial expectations? It is caring for people. The most important reason for becoming a physician should not be financial gain. This is a hard idea in a society that believes this goal is all right for everyone else. In order for medicine to be rewarding in this country, one must rise above that notion. The primary reason for going into this area of sacrifice must be helping and healing the illness of humanity.

Is it not interesting, however, that medical school enrollment is down? The GPA requirement to get in is as well. Case in point is that this country has been built on the idea that if one is willing to sacrifice and work hard, one will reap the capitalist rewards. This opportunity was created by our forefathers as they fought for freedom and that right. However, John Adams warned it would fail with a loss of moral compass. Without morality and integrity, capitalism leaves room for greed and corruption, but in other societies that envy us, how is it better? Is socialism perfect? Is communism? Is being under the rule of a dictator? There still seems to be the idea that these are not any better, at least to most. The effort of many immigrants to come here should be proof enough. If physicians are to be content, they must rise above this capitalist notion and consider their role as something more than a vehicle for financial gain. Is that fair? Is that for the best? I will leave it to you to answer.

I have been my happiest in this world, which is in need of empathy and compassion, when I have ignored financial concerns and moved into the arena of giving, caring, and loving. That is how it has worked for me. Ironically, I was trained as an anesthesiologist and went on to specialized training in the practice of pain management. I say it was ironic because my personal life has been a mirror image of the pain I have treated. Day after day and year after year of administering ER, OB, and trauma anesthesia, I have served the depressed, emotionally spent, drained, physically tormented souls who suffer with constant pain—so many painful conditions that I could write an entire book on the subject. If I ever did, it would not be like some I have read. It would be a case-by-case study of those who have lived and died in pain—their stories and the impacts they should have had but didn't.

All we see on television are the effects of drug abuse on those who take prescribed drugs for purposes outside their intended use, along with the use of illicit drugs. How much do we see of the people who are able to walk, play with their grandchildren, go grocery shopping, and have full, functional lives, no longer suffering the constant agony of pain because of their responsible use of medication prescribed by caring physicians and taken as directed? In some cases they even remain viably employed.

I have rejoiced for those with malignant pain only because an end was coming. They didn't have to defend their right to die with dignity. I have suffered along with benign-chronic pain patients as they struggled to live on while having someone care without judgment. The pain is not life threatening but they will suffer from it the remainder of their lives. I have encountered many who have been treated with procedure after procedure that failed to offer any long-term benefits. Often they would attempt to justify their pain so they would not be labeled as weak, pathetic, drug-addicted patients. Sadly there was no need for their frustration as it should be obvious to any skilled clinician familiar with pain management that the reasons for the pain were justified.

I have performed procedures. I have placed opiate pumps and spinal stimulators to try to block pain and move away from the daily oral dosing of opiates. I've sent patients to spine surgeons with hopes for outcomes that would negate the need for further medications. There were successes, and there were failures. In the end there were times when I was left with no choice but to medicate or allow suffering.

Drug screens are taken. State tracking is used. Those of us in this difficult field try to do what we can to stop the abuse. Still, one is left wondering how many of the righteous have to suffer for the sins of the wicked.

One thing I cannot understand is if one does become a pain specialist, how can that doctor not prescribe anything in an effort to help? How does he or she leave that with the primary-care physician? If you have never suffered from pain, how can you understand? Still, it has been a bitter pill for me to swallow when patients have abused what I have given them. One stole my script pad and wrote narcotics on my license until he was caught. It's hard to go on from there and attend to the needs of legitimate patients.

As an ER physician, I ran many codes for cardiac arrest. I faced many families to tell them their loved ones did not make it. I dealt with perverts in the middle of the night who had placed objects in places only a surgeon could remove. There is no training to fully prepare one to work in the ER—or to be a physician at all, in my opinion. In high-risk trauma anesthesia, I have had more than one teenager die on the table while I gave it all I had. I have seen an OB C-section go well under my skill only to have the mother die in front of me with an amniotic fluid embolism before she got to hold her newborn, even as I was telling her how beautiful her baby was.

So you tell me what I am worth. Will I ever receive an Oscar? Will I ever win an NBA title or wear a World Series ring? I will not. I won't wear the lightweight championship belt that I might have. Who knew it would be possible to be worshipped and paid more to beat people than to help them?

We as physicians pay the price. Don't get me wrong. I have met more than one physician I am embarrassed to have as my colleague. Then again, maybe some feel that way about me. Is it not that way in any profession? Also, this is not only about my feelings regarding medicine. Society does not, in my opinion, see the value in teachers, police officers, or firefighters—and a list of others. Ironically, there came a time I was so disappointed with medicine that I applied and was interviewed for acceptance into the police academy. The goal was to be a Texas Ranger. I only recently tossed the application and the card of the officer who interviewed me and offered me the opportunity. It was legit.

I had convinced myself I would be happier in this line of work. Perhaps it was just a midlife crisis, as I was older at the time. Why didn't I take the job? Change. Risk. Money. The children still had needs, and I could fill them easier, it seemed, by holding on as a physician. I acknowledge that other professions do not get paid what they deserve. I quite frankly could not offer or do for my children financially the same in police work as in medicine, despite all I written about my disappointments with medicine. The current risk in being a police officer needs no explanation.

I am confident that in one form or another, I was guilty of providing too much materially. Would I have been happier as a Texas Ranger? Would my children truly have been better off? Perhaps in some ways, but not in others. In trying to explain my thoughts regarding the choice of medicine, I do believe I need to point out that a time came when I could have gotten out, yet I chose to stay put—maybe not for me so much but for those I loved. My son was in trouble at the time, and I considered his needs and my ability to be there for him. His troubles were real enough. They continued for better than a decade. I am his father. Love dictated I remain available to do what I could, whether it was too much or not enough.

I have mentioned it takes many years to become a physician. Most of us spend all our twenties and even a few good years into the thirties. That doesn't count paying back the debt. I think most feel the reward will be in the eventual independence of running one's own practice. Instead, with the changes in medicine and insurance, many have become employees of hospitals or large groups, and with that comes drama—getting along with others and being subjected to what they expect. The job is only as good as your boss.

This can be good but also rather bad, to the point that the physician decides to move to what he or she hopes will be greener pastures. I have experienced this more than once. It is very discouraging, but greed is usually part of the decision. Along with quality of care at its worst, even legal battles can occur, and no matter the verdict the cost is high. I have experienced that. I have felt vindicated yet spent. It was an emotional and financial drain. These experiences remind me of winning the Golden Gloves. That night after the fight, I sat on the couch for several hours with my ears ringing due to the blows I had taken. I looked at the trophy and then my wife, who was checking on me. I remember asking, "Tamara, are you sure I won?"

This chapter is devoted to the suffering. The emotionally lost. The physically spent. The people I treated and even those whose funerals I spoke at (at the families' request). Those I loved. Those who blessed me. Those who gave me the privilege even when I had to overcome the honest resentment I felt when I was paid less than the contractor who had built their houses. In the end it didn't matter. What mattered was that in the midst of this, I still cared. What matters is that you do, as well. We will leave this world with nothing. Was this chapter enough to make you think? I hope so. Think about what you hold important and what you don't.

I cannot say I was ever able to recommend this profession to my children. I felt the price was just too much to pay. As much as I cared for and was blessed to help others, the toll it took over the years was more than I can explain. I shared my troubles in preceding chapters to explain why I felt that way. Certainly it is a lesson in sacrifice and love. The pay is still better than most jobs. The stress and consumption of one's energy are definitely a lot to endure. Most people look forward to retirement. That may never come for me. I believe I will have to work part time. I am blessed to have a profession that can allow that. Some fortunate people find things they love so much, they cannot imagine doing anything else until they die. Many singers and actors do that. Again, a lesson in love and in loving what you do. Fatigue has given me enough pause to think of other things. If I advised my children poorly, all that remains is asking for their forgiveness, which I have.

Sleeping under the stars. A bonfire without thought of work. Hiking within the wonder of nature. Riding a horse and having the time to care for it. Sitting by a warm fire and having the energy to chop the wood that went into it. Writing about life and other things, realizing there is no need to watch the clock. The gift of love can be measured in the joy of living without ever looking at something as a job but rather as a journey of love. It seems this reality is harder in some careers and easier in others. Looking forward to retirement would appear to be driven by fatigue. What a blessing to not really ever feel that way. Yet if one does at times, there is an option: to continue with purpose and drive to make the world a better place.

It is good to trust in a higher power, to believe there is meaning in what one does, in investing in and giving to others. If habits can be learned, it certainly is of value to learn this one. Don't let the blindness of negativity create the experience rather than learning to enjoy the ride. And again, learning to do what? Love. To trust despite ourselves the gift of giving is the gift itself.

If there are those who believe you chose poorly, that another path would have served you better and not been as hard on your feet, finish strong! Let love push you on. What you chose doesn't define you anyway. You are like me: here for only a short while. Most of us will not be mentioned in history. For those who are, the truth is just that—they are only mentioned. Some a little, others more. Yet no matter how much, there is an end to it. Let us through love strive for eternity. No beginning. No end. All of us now becoming more than a notion. A great deal more than mere mention. Sons and daughters of a universe created by love.

Are you like me? A brief thought? A mere mention? An autobiography? Perhaps you are like others more famous or known, recorded in history. No matter. Whichever you are, it is all right. Only love matters. It is all that will last beyond the grave.

CHAPTER 9

FAMILY

A happy family feels like home

Through love all that is bitter will be sweet
Through love all that is copper will be gold.
Through love all dregs will turn to purest wine
Through love all pain will turn to medicine.

—*Rumi*

As stressful as families can be, I think most will agree they are one of the most important things this side of eternity. Most families have at least one child who is prone to trouble and strife. There is a giant leap from lying on the couch with three little ones watching *Lady and the Tramp* to the time the phone call comes from the police. One child has grown up enough to wear orange and talk to you through glass. From Disney World with cartoon characters to memories that are not pleasant at all.

The pain of this can be enormous. It seems many of the patients I have treated through the years who had such pain in their lives and suffered great losses were the ones who had the most mercy. There is a lack of kindness from some who stand in judgment and voice harsh and crude things such as "We have all have trouble. You need to get over the pity party. You're bringing me down!" Sharing these things with selfish so-called free spirits is a mistake. I think it is true that very few are spared pain while living here, and no doubt some handle the pain better than others. There are those who have good runs in life. They are blessed. I think they should pause, though, before they pass judgment on those less fortunate. It is clear that drowning in sorrow offers no relief. People all have their own ways of grieving, and I am unaware of a definitive time limit.

My residency was over, and it was time to find a place to work and to pay back money I had borrowed for school. A time to raise the kids and, hopefully, give the woman I had married a life that was beyond the hell of medical school and the twenty-dollar wedding we'd had. She had earned it by staying by my side and giving me three kids.

After a short time in Virginia, which we fled after the hospital where I worked was taken to task for Medicare fraud, we relocated to Southern Missouri. This started off well, and we had a run of five good years before it collapsed. Tamara and I worked on getting out of debt from school and kept our living expenses down. I took on the responsibly of directing three very good certified registered nurse anesthetists. I worked in the ER when administration needed me and developed epidural care for those in the labor of childbirth. Administration and the staff of surgeons were all friendly.

After we paid off the debt, Tamara and I treated the kids to Disney World and ourselves to a trip I am so thankful we took. Although our wedding hadn't been much, the love between us was. So after ten years, Tamara asked what I would like to do for our anniversary. I had not been out of the country. I asked to go wherever it was that Marlon Brando had made *Mutiny on the Bounty*. I didn't even know where it was. Not too long after that, we were on our way to French Polynesia. It was quite a leap from not having been out of the country to traveling that far. Overall it was a beautiful experience, and we met great friends who were celebrating their anniversary as well. We spent most of the time with Henry and Rhonda.

The islands of Bora Bora and Moorea were quite beautiful. Still, there was evidence we were still on earth, and the tropical paradise was not without flaw. I found that out with a shellfish surprise and ended up with food poisoning that resulted in running for cover every time I was forced to "express myself." Also, we were snorkeling and wondering why all the beautiful fish were gathered in one place, only to discover a sewage pipe nearby. This caused a rapid surface and spitting out all the water I could! Still, what I would give to return! I had youth and a woman who loved me. The sewage wouldn't bother me now.

The point is, you should enjoy as much of this planet as you can, especially with those you love, for you never know when it will end. Tamara and I would never get to travel again, as it turned out. Tragedy was lurking like the sharks beneath the reef in Brando's land of wonder. The bite would be vicious and terminal.

I wish sometimes that whenever I look back, there would be some force or power that would slap the shit out of me and make me turn around. Play the hand that was dealt. Not expend useless energy on swimming— or, rather, drowning—in the past. Choices. Decisions. The benefit of wisdom and hindsight. In the name of merciful God! We do what we do and base it on the information we have at the time. Later, more information comes and creates regret. How can that be productive? What is done is done. I do understand this. One could not pay me a million dollars for the memories in this chapter. Well, perhaps several million... Hey! I am only human! Ha!Ha! But no. Tamara, I am glad we had that time together.

Are we happy with the finished product? Did we leave this world shining bright or with a dull notion of what might have been? I believe this is what frames us. This is success or failure. This is love.

Time passes so quickly. You move through it. The joy amid the pain. One is young and strong. Believing in another chance. Better cards. Suddenly there is the mirror. You're older. You're just old. Another chance? Any more cards to be played? Are the dice loaded? Did the captain lie, like the poet and songwriter Leonard Cohen suggests in his song, "Everybody Knows"?

So many have expressed that life without love is rather worthless. I also have heard it expressed that success without fulfillment is not success at all. There's also the notion that success and achievement revolve around a scientific formula composed of almost 100 percent love.

For Tamara and me, there was no knowing what was coming. Marty Robbins reminded me of it in a song, "You Gave Me a Mountain": "You know, Lord, I've been in a prison / for something that I've never done. / It's been one hill after another, / but I've climbed them all, one by one. / But this time, Lord, you gave me a mountain, / a mountain I may never climb. / And it isn't a hill any longer. / You gave me a mountain this time." A mountain was coming. I can say to this day I continue to climb every day to the best of my ability.

The glue that holds us firm at times is family. Much of this idea is lost in present society. Families are broken, divorced, and lost. We should hold on to one another as much as love will allow.

Recently, at a family reunion, I observed a very large family that had held on to one another despite losses and difficulties. Even those who were no longer married came to express care for the family despite the differences that had pushed them apart. I sat quietly in a chair, simply watching. Despite the differences, the varied opinions, they came together and celebrated life. There was love. They danced. Some drank, but there was no fighting. Just laughter and love. Through it all they had remained intact, recognizing the need for family despite their problems here in this life. Despite numerous losses and fatigue, I did try to hang on to the concept of family the best I could. I tried very hard to maintain the integrity that only family can give to my children. It was not easy. Thank God for the love of their grandparents.

I love to think of us in the hereafter: One huge family. A family bound together through endless love. That we remain. Forever! You're not alone when broken by the loss of family. Perhaps, like me, you've had the sense that you never had the love of a family, at least not for long. Let it go. Don't dwell on it, for there is no love in that! Love now. That is all you have left. This is a daily task. No matter your story regarding family, it is your privilege to love as much as possible.

CHAPTER 10

LOVE

Building on love not loss

Absence sharpens love, presence strengthens it.

—*Thomas Fuller*

*The love of family and the admiration of
friends is much more important than wealth
and privilege.*

—*Charles Kuralt*

After these times of joy and feeling that youth would
be ours forever, with the reward finally arriving—
this reward earned through sacrifice—suddenly the
conversation changed to how to we would live life from
there. The country life seemed to be agreeing with the

family, and Tamara and I could think of worse things than horses, acres, timber, and walks with the dogs through the grass and trees. After the school debts were paid, we gave it some time. Since my job was going well, perhaps it was time to build a home. Since we were debt free, we could have chosen anything. Back to the military? A move to a larger city where the kids might have more opportunities, good or bad? I could take a job for less money but perhaps more benefits?

Tamara was well liked there. She was active in the community and making a difference. She and I even provided entertainment for hospital banquets. After much consideration, we finally decided to stay where we were. We eventually chose to go forward with building a home. Tamara designed it herself. We selected a custom builder. Soon the stone and brick were taking form. The fireplaces were made from cut stone. The walls and roof were just about to take shape. We planned for my father and her folks, for when the days came when they might need care. No one wanted them to be anywhere but with us. I wanted Tamara to be pleased, and she sure planned a beautiful castle, complete with Italian marble and Spanish tile, a glass shower, and even a safe room. All of it was coming together, and after what we had been through, it seemed nothing less than magical.

I was standing at the scrub sink at the hospital getting ready for the next case when the message came. I was told my wife was waiting just outside recovery. I mentioned Tamara was well thought of, for she volunteered at just about everything and had been instrumental in helping to rebuild the town's old theater into a playhouse. She'd even helped put on a couple of productions there. When she came to the hospital, she was always welcome.

I went through the doors to recovery, and there she stood: the love of my life and the mother of my three children. Tears were running down her face, and I immediately thought something had happened to the children. They were fine, but she was not. The words came from her mouth like those of a drunk who'd had one too many.

I heard her words but couldn't accept them. They caused my spine to shake and my heart to break at the same time. She had cancer. In a moment it all came crashing down. As a physician I was all too familiar with the term and what it could likely bring. I could see it all like a tape on fast-forward. There was nothing I could think of except to look up and ask God, "Why now?" After all Tamara and I had made it—survived medical school and the births of three children. Our school debts were paid. We were young, and this was to be our time: A time to enjoy all the dreams we had imagined. A new home and a renewed life together that was as close to perfect as a young family could have! Of course, the answer did not come, not then nor since.

Tamara had fibrocystic disease, and she had delayed getting a second opinion regarding the mass until I insisted. She had been seen by a friend and colleague who believed the lump was nothing to be concerned about. So now the news came as a shock. I held her and told her it would be all right. She wouldn't die! But I knew breast cancer in a young woman was rarely good. In a matter of seconds, I saw myself a widower with three young children. Neither of us had any idea of how we would tell the kids or explain it.

We went home and spent the rest of the evening crying, praying, and wondering how only a day before, the most important thing had been building a new home. Now that home was worth nothing, and I thought of how it could be a tomb for her to die in. After seeing my parents lose their home during my younger years, I recalled how badly I had wanted to replace it. Somehow I was again fooled into believing this was security and certainty. Striving for these things can lead only to misery, for the only security here is that there is none. The only certainty is the lack of any.

I remember meeting the contractor working on our home out on the acres where it was being built. He said he had some bad news for me: he had underbid the home, and it was going to cost $100,000 more than he had thought. This was more than just a small mistake. He had given us a bid on three different occasions. He gave many excuses and reasons, but in the end all I could say was, "You have bad news for me? My wife has cancer. What else can you really tell me?"

This was grossly unfair at the least. I do have to admit he seemed to present his mistake with the voice and manner of honesty. To this day I am uncertain as to his integrity regarding the matter. It is for him to take to his grave. There was and is no value in my continuing to wonder. Naturally, with all that was happening, my thoughts were far from clear at the time—emotions unchecked creating unsound reasoning. I gained what clarity I could with the passing of time.

The nightmare began. First it was the mastectomy, followed by chemotherapy, since the cancer was in her lymph nodes. The radiation seemed to do more damage than good. When my wife was taken into surgery for removal of her breasts, she started crying, I stood helplessly by and thought, *Why so much suffering in the world, God?* It means much more when it becomes personal.

I went to the banker and told him I didn't want the house. It was too late, and the state we were in was one of two that did not require contractors to carry builders' risk insurance, according to an attorney I consulted. I would be covering the shortfall with yet another debt. I knew this would turn into a financial disaster. I was never fond of involvement in legal matters despite being encouraged to do so regarding my colleague who had not ordered a biopsy. He was remorseful, and I was weary and confused. At the time I failed to comprehend the benefit. He was a friend, and I chose not to put either of us through additional stress. There was an element of peace obtained in knowing Tamara would see her new home before God called her to her true one.

The cancer spread at the speed of sound—the sound of pain. As it invaded her bones, the agony overcame us. Her oncologist had concerns about addiction to opiates—something I have never understood to this day. I sought other options. As the drugs escalated, we had to deal with all the issues of tolerance and dependence, which are not the same as addiction. I was the only one in the rural area who knew about pain and associated medications. Tamara became unable to travel without increased pain. I attempted to adjust the medication to lessen the horror. I made an attempt to shelter the children from this harsh reality.

I don't remember when we moved into the home. Tamara smiled, seeing what she had created. The joy was short lived, though, for we knew what was unfolding: three little ones and me in this palace, with no mother. I couldn't see us staying there after she was gone. It is wise not to make these decisions too soon, but I made the decision the day we moved in. I reemphasize the difficulties in making logical decisions when emotional chaos defies logic. I needed someone to turn to who had the children's and my best interest at heart. I was confused greatly. Those I did turn to in time created more confusion and pain.

I have looked once again in the rearview mirror regarding this choice, thinking perhaps the children and I should have stayed, if for no other reason than to grieve properly. I think it's fair to say my love for Tamara was proven by my insanity after she was gone. Right or wrong I concluded the beautiful home wasn't worth much without her in it.

There is something I want to say about this process. I pray I can write it with humility and fairness. Tamara did not simply accept this diagnosis and pass it off as fate. She fought like a true warrior. She rebuked it, and I joined her. We fought it with every alternative care method I could find, with faith, and with prayer. We gave thanks for the victory over pain and death. We utilized laughter. Her strength was a testimony, her endurance majestic. We fought it together as hard as we could. We fought it for us. We fought it for our children.

In the process of claiming victory, there were those who questioned her faith due to the lack of physical healing. Perhaps it was more my faith they questioned. How could anyone believe a physician could accept cancer could be cured by a means outside of standard treatment? It was difficult for me, but not impossible. The courage Tamara revealed daily for the children was nothing less than a testimony of her strength. The time came, however, that as her husband, I ensured that anyone who questioned her lack of physical healing for whatever reason simply stopped. My prayers changed. Petitions for physical healing were exchanged with pleas for an end to the suffering. The suffering was too much to bear. A higher power had the final say. From hospice, the church, and all else, it became obvious the end was coming. The pain became difficult to control with oral and IV meds alone. Travel was an option no longer. Being isolated in a rural area didn't help. I was trained and credentialed in the placement of intraspinal pumps. We were hours away from anyone else of similar training. It was a procedure more than a surgery. The hospital believed it appropriate for me to offer this form of treatment to Tamara. I took my wife to surgery and implanted an opiate pump. This device would allow morphine to be delivered directly to her spine. I placed the device with precision and ease. With changes in medical treatment laws regarding family in the last decade, I doubt this would be allowed today.

I had started a pain clinic for the hospital and was trained in pain medicine. Considering all the factors and the limited choices, medical decisions were left to me. I would have preferred not to have it this way. The staff was supportive to the extent of their training, which brings me to consider what we could have done. Travel to the closest metropolitan area for treatment and care from another specialist? At that stage of her disease, we believed this option would place an unreasonable burden on her. It was far too painful. Tamara desired to die in the home she had built.

During the procedure I injected dye to check placement of the spinal catheter and discovered yet another mass: a tumor on the cord. It was cutting her in half. At that moment her being partially paralyzed made sense.

It was only to get worse. Out of the hospital, we went back to our dream home to face the nightmare to come.

The day came when Tamara hit the floor. She would never use her walker again. From that time on, she was totally paralyzed from the waist down. We placed a hospital bed in the living area so she could visualize most of the home.

I was still working at the hospital. At home people from our local church and nursing care rotated during the day until I could get there to assist as needed. The hospital stayed true to me for a time during this period, and it was never mentioned that I was wavering in my medical duties. Eventually the time came when I was told it would most likely be better if I stayed home with her until her suffering was over. I understood the reasoning, considering the risk of my working in surgery. Financially, the hospital's position was unsatisfactory at best. Telling me to take a leave of absence without pay was rather cruel in my opinion. I don't remember a conversation about short-term disability. My inability to process all that was happening was another of life's lightning strikes that limited my ability to reason. I walked out. Years later others informed me I should have made them fire me and then sued them. I maintain the mind can only process so much information at any one time. Like a computer that crashes, the ability to reason and display sound judgment is impaired. The owner of a local clinic offered me work out of mercy.

That enabled me to get through until Tamara's end came.

I worked very hard while employed at the hospital, regarding my duties and development of services. There was a change in administration. At first they called in anesthesia help to provide support during this difficult time. The help turned out to be someone wanting to replace me and using the tragedy as a means of doing it. Then something strange happened. There was talk of narcotics missing from the OR. With what I was enduring, I apparently became suspect. The state was called in, and after a few meetings and drug screens, it became obvious it wasn't me. Later, the guilty party was discovered. From what I was told, it was the very person who was hired to be my support. This was hearsay. I will never know the entire truth. I do know the entire process hurt me very much. Though I was limited in my ability to reason regarding what I should do after Tamara's death, the idea of my return to the hospital didn't appeal to me at the time. To my credit, I am proud I had the courage to take the children elsewhere for a fresh start. The children have shared with me that they were thankful for the move and a new beginning. I did have the presence of mind to believe blaming others wouldn't bring Tamara back. Perhaps down deep inside, I wished even then to offer love and forgiveness despite the emotional pain.

During the last few months of her life, Tamara never complained. She never was angry, or if she was, she never revealed it. She read her Bible and praised God for her chance to be with him if it was not his will for a physical healing. It broke my heart. I do understand a broken heart.

There is no intent to disrespect my wife or her memory. Quite the opposite. The reason I offer details is to confirm the message of this writing. My wife loved everyone throughout this horrific battle. She gave it and accepted it. The verdict is simple enough: love can prevail and provide healing, even in a situation like this. I failed to do this on occasion. I was angry. I cursed on one occasion, I recall. Tamara never did. Love overcame death. The time I lacked love did not help me heal.

The kids and I camped with tent and lantern outside the bedroom window. I relocated Tamara's bed so she could enjoy the children. We made a fire and hot dogs, and she laughed as she watched us climb trees and play hide-and-seek. I don't know what held me up, but it must have been the arms of a higher power despite the anger I had revealed.

The night came. Earlier she had asked me to prepare her a bowl of popcorn—her favorite comfort food. She ate it and then called everyone to her bedside—her friends and parents and other family. It was her time to say goodbye. The tumor had invaded her diaphragm, and she was having seizures and choking. Many people wonder why horrible things happen to them. Others with ego and pride boast and brag about what greatness they have earned or worked for. Sure, people work for things. But in the end, nothing belongs to you. It is a simple rule: you are blessed to have or have not. Anything can be taken in a heartbeat. Where is all the bragging and boasting then? Suddenly those who have lost are forced to reinvent themselves, and they sometimes choose to become humble and less self-centered people. There is a new theme. They realize it really wasn't all about them. Timing and circumstance had parts to play. The bragging is gone. The childish, egocentric behavior as well.

One thing I am ever puzzled by. There are many who indicate they obtained their success through hard work and persistence. I have no doubt of the truth in that. My question remains: What is to be said for the countless others who did the same but without the same outcome? My belief is there were times for most of these success stories when productivity met opportunity. The hard work had to be there, but so did an opportunity at the right time that provided that needed lift to the next level. Perhaps it's not always the case. Yet I think it is the case more often than it's noted. Most of us get by with a little help from our friends, as Lennon and McCartney declared in song.

Tamara and I had our last talk. She told me she wished she had shown me more love. It was not until these times that we had a firm grasp on how unconditional our love was. Through the years, we purchased many cards and flowers for each other. Medical school had not been easy, and at times our love was tested. We had worked through any issues, however, and resolved them. We had been our happiest before her illness came.

Her fight to live was courageous. It was unfortunate that by the time death was inevitable, she was clouded in mind by medication. She was unable to give me clear instructions for her wishes regarding the children. I was left disorientated and confused. Over the years, thank God, I finally forgave myself for the mistakes I made in raising them. I decided to accept that love was greatly involved. I gave it my best.

We had our last kiss. A seizure came. I asked God to let it be the last one. It was. My heart broke into pieces. For myself and our children. For her mother and father standing by. For all of us! She asked me for one last favor: to watch over our son, Taylor. He would be the one to have trouble, she said. I don't know how she knew. Maybe she figured he would be angry, but even at the end she had her motherly instinct. I did what she asked and have all these years.

The children were kept at a friend's during these final moments in an attempt to spare them from memories that could scar them for years. I realize the courage Tamara showed was *a gift* to them. It was her attempt to let *love* prevail over agonizing *fear.* After she passed, I had the children brought over so they could see her for the last time in this life.

The children were young and innocent. They recall their limited understanding at the time of this heartbreaking loss and the fear that certainly attempted to enter them. It became apparent that love remained. I am confident to this day they believe they will be in the presence of their mother again. Each had his or her individual reaction. My heart broke for them. However, each held me up as much as I did them. I will not comment on the matter further.

Tamara wanted me to preach at the funeral, so I did. I had my boxing trainer come in to work my corner again. Terry gave me strength, as he had in the ring before. There were nearly a thousand people there. Tamara had been an inspiration to so many. I had many things to say, but in the end, it was about what she had meant to us, and about the healing that finally came—not in our way but in God's. Despite the tragedy, at least I had known what it was to be loved by a woman and give it back in return. Many never have that. For that I was blessed.

With the help of the associate pastor who joined in, I struggled through "Go Rest High on That Mountain" by Vince Gill. Tamara was placed six feet deep in an old country cemetery, one she had chosen months before. It was peaceful, with an old oak tree close by. A small place, what she liked. I remember going with her to look at it. That's not a date anyone would care to plan for.

As I went forth, there was no room for getting over it. There was only to live with it. People who have said things to me like "Get over it," I find, have not had much tragedy in their lives. It is not possible, I think, for those who really love. I think it's more reasonable to live with it better each day.

Through the years, on many sleepless nights, I have been reminded of Tamara's smile and the love I lost. There are three songs that always come to mind. First is Bonnie Raitt's "Wounded Heart."

Wounded heart, I cannot save you from yourself
Though I wanted to be brave, it never helped
Cause your trouble's like a flood raging through
your veins
No amount of love's enough to end the pain
Tenderness and time can heal a right gone wrong
But the anger that you feel goes on and on
And it's not enough to know that I love you still
So I'll take my heart and go, for I've had my fill

The Boss—Bruce Springsteen—writes and sings "If I Should Fall Behind."

We said we'd walk together, baby, come what may
That come the twilight should we lose our way
If as we're walking a hand should slip free
I'll wait for you
And should I fall behind
Wait for me...
Now everyone dreams of love lasting and true
Oh, but you and I know what this world can do

So let's make our steps clear that the other may
see...

Now there's a beautiful river in the valley ahead
There 'neath the oak's bough soon we will be
wed
Should we lose each other in the shadow of the
evening trees
I'll wait for you
Should I fall behind
Wait for me

Last, but certainly not least, is my daughter's song. She
was gifted with her mother's incredible voice. She wrote
a song for Tamara called "Eternity." It was her first (and,
I pray, not her last) CD and music video. It was featured
in the movie I produced about some of these truths
wrapped in a web of fiction called *Between Heaven and
Hell.*

I wait for you
Seems like an eternity
That night I had to let you go
My heart sinks from the memory
I push away the thought of how your hand could
slip from mine
Why this pain has been brought
As we were at the doors of paradise

Your heart seems so far, but side by side our souls
will never part
Remaining in me
A love for eternity
I need your courage now
In that I know I can confide
Remembering how you loved me
Your real eyes, they never lied
Now the best of every day is when I lay down my
head at night
Into my dreams a beautiful light

I know I have a fighting chance if I hold you deep
inside
Though I cannot see your face, nothing is more
alive
You're the strongest voice when all the angels sing
Your heart seems so far
Side by side, our souls will never part
Remaining in me our love for eternity
I wait for you
Seems like an eternity

I marvel that through it all, I went on to treat pain. After
all these years, I still am shocked at what people have
endured. What they have been through. How they have
stood up under it all. They will never be stars. They will
never win any awards. They exist nonetheless. They

were the ones who lived with pain, their pride and ego stripped by tragedy and loss. Perhaps that is the divine purpose of it. Holy books present as much. I feel worse for those who, in their blind ignorance, think their youth and vanity will last. They are chasing after the wind. It will not. The wind will blow. It will all be left behind and perhaps not be mentioned much. Even if their achievements were high, they will still be memories. Just like all of us.

Of course, some leave more of a mark in history than others. If that were not true, there would be far less to write about, and no history classes. Some are remembered for greatness, others for terrible things they did to humanity. Wars and rumors of them. Heroes that resulted from them. Greatness in music or politics. Hollywood. Sports. However, death is the great equalizer in the end. Great or small. Remembered or forgotten. Not here. Not present. All gone. Not love, though. It is the emotion that is looked for. Fought for! In this life and beyond, it remains powerful and true. Evil and hatred make countless efforts to drown it out. Yet love remains!

Before Tamara was paralyzed, before her hair was gone and a scarf adorned her head, I took her to Branson, Missouri, where she saw them all: Campbell, Clark, Andy Williams, Johnny and June, and her first love, Jerry Reed. Johnny and June held the children after the show. Jerry waited for all others to leave and had Tamara sit on his lap on the steps of his camper for fifteen minutes. How gracious they were to her, filled with love and compassion. I can say I was in the front row with her when Johnny and June performed "Ring of Fire." I felt the fire. I felt it burn. I looked at Tamara and back at Johnny and June. Words failed me. What I can say is I could swear I smelled the smoke as well as my flesh burning. There was a ring of fire, and it consumed me. My darling was dying, and the fire burned. It burned. I felt the flames. I felt the pain.

Decades later my son wrote a song, *"The Hand of Pain."* We had been dealt the hand of pain. I am confident most of you have had these most terrible of times. If not, you will. All you can do is keep on breathing. You are left to ask and answer for yourself not only why, but, if you had known it was coming, whether you would choose to repeat it. Well, we did love. We were given the chance to experience it. To live beside it. To sleep with it. Despite the agony and defeat of loss here on earth, we had the chance to get a glimpse of what love is, the difference it makes. This love gave me the chance, as it did you: the chance to be better, at least for a moment, than anything we might have been without it. Our situation was no doubt terrible and could have left anyone lost and insane. Love did give it purpose. Love is the key to remaining sane.

In honesty, as a mere human, I didn't believe I needed this loss. I wasn't sure if I had or had not done anything to deserve it. Why did I have these thoughts? Because I had learned to be afraid. After my mother, this experience with my wife and the mother of my children would leave me to fight for my sanity. Trying to go on with three children to raise on my own is not something I would have chosen. The years to come would cause me to ponder why I had married or had children at all, to think about an easier way: A pension. Retirement. Less pressure. These thoughts, I discovered, were reasonable, and forgiveness for them was not needed. It is part of the grieving process, I believe. Dwelling on them is counterproductive.

Getting trapped in the past of choices already made is a no-win for anyone. I have been able to see there is little love in it. I have also gained the wisdom to see that without all that has occurred, I would be less able to give, receive, or understand the concept of love. If all that has happened to you has made you what you are, then either love who you are or let love change you so you can.

I shared this with you not asking you to compare. I am not keeping score and asking whether your story is better or worse. It is only a story. It is mine. Yours is yours. Different. I think some fear they have no story. Everyone does. It is yours and no one else's. Make the most of it. Recall your record. Look in the mirror and forgive. Love. Walk away loving what you see. There are no do-overs, and even if there were, would any of us truthfully be better off? We will never know. Love commands you to accept what is. Love yourself enough to do this. It will be difficult at times. Some of us have committed great wrongs. I can say that continually beating yourself will not allow you the chance to love again. I get it! I know! I have beaten myself into a coma. Love allows me to regain consciousness. It will for you as well.

CHAPTER 11
EMOTIONS
Guarding the heart and mind

*Love involves a peculiar unfathomable
combination of understanding and
misunderstanding.*

—*Diane Arbus*

There I was with three children. No helpmate to counsel with. How was I to be Mother and Dad? We were in a home where we had experienced an enormous amount of sorrow. I had been hurt by decisions the hospital made after Tamara became ill. I understood the need for me to go home and wait until death came. Of course they felt there was risk with me doing my duties under this pressure. I questioned the manner in which it was handled. No short-term disability? Children and a house? The humiliation.

Many will say, "Don't do anything fast. Let some time go by." Surely there would be another woman I could help, and she could help me. A replacement mom? A replacement spouse? How ridiculous to allow these thoughts too soon! My mental state was overrun with emotion and not truth. Fiction, not reality. I had no time to grieve in an effective way. No place to go and stay for refuge. No time to grieve. There were children and school. It is a hard lesson to realize that waiting a few months here or there could have saved years of agony. I needed time to get my bearings, but there was no time. The house had to be dealt with: The debt of it. The burden that surrounded it. I can say that the choices I made during that time only added to the cost. I attempted to get involved with an old girlfriend from decades earlier who had had her own share of disaster. I wanted to see what had happened to her through the years. That inquiry was not given enough thought. She needed help with her daughter. I certainly was at a loss. Trying to force this before a more appropriate time was absurd and foolish. It turned into more trouble than I already had.

The saddest was the involvement of innocent children. I most likely will never completely forgive myself for that weak round in what was to be a fight for my life and sanity. I believe I should forgive myself. There is no love in not doing so. I was broken, and my need for help combined with emotional upheaval surpassed my ability to reason—a. Another of life's lightning strikes that altered me.

It's interesting how the circle continues. My old love had known my mother well. In fact, she indicated she was a lot like Mother. I should have listened more to that comment! I mentioned why my mother had given me my name. This woman explained she had given her daughter my middle name as well. After me. This was very hard to believe, especially after I found out her natural father had the same middle name! I found this ironic considering my mother's explanation to me as to how she had given me the same middle name after another man she claimed to love.

I cannot dignify it with a long explanation. It was a mistake and resulted in shame and guilt. Why? Because there was no love in it. At the time there was rather a spirit of selfishness. Some things said and done can be described only as bad tempered and mean. What can be said is that for some people, there is no restraint when it comes to taking advantage of another, especially when one is hurting and crippled by despair. People do prey on the misfortune of others. These are not kind people. There was no need to inflict more pain on either of us. This shouldn't have happened. It was based on emotional instability and not logical reasoning.

I could attempt to offer excuses and to blame her. But this is worthless. I did need time to grieve, and there was no tolerance for it. Yet with two sides to every coin, why bother with futile explanations? In short, it's better to take the higher road and accept my involvement in the matter All of us should take accountability for our actions. Yet what good does it do to blame ourselves continually? Sure, we need to learn from our mistakes. There is the time to love enough to move on, however. We either do that or realize we are unable to move at all—frozen forever. I do hope she was able to love and find love. I certainly pray her daughter turned out well. That she was able to heal and find love. That her daughter and her father were given time together rather than increased distance and strife.

That short and ugly relationship was dissolved, and I placed the house on the auction block. The children and I left to start over in Texas. After a time, all that was left of the acreage and life in Missouri was the memory of the loss that had occurred.

My ex-girlfriend called a few times, and I attempted to speak with reason, but the wounds were too fresh. In time I chose to forgive us both, again choosing love. I never felt good about calling her again, however. I have to admit I believe love can allow us to leave some things alone. Sure, it would be better to be able to sit face to face with all those we have hurt or who have hurt us, giving each the opportunity to love and forgive. As a human, and realizing the condition of humanity, I have to be truthful and state that trying to give and accept forgiveness before the other party is ready can leave things worse than they had been. Regarding these matters, I can only advise with thought and reflection that you make the best choice you can.

The cards had been dealt, and I was left to play the hand. There was no way out, no asking for a better hand. This was what happened. There was no changing it.

The new beginning in Texas was far from easy. I was a forty-year-old man. Gone were the days of being able to move with everything I owned in the back seat of my car. Where was the book, some sort of guide on how to be a mother and a father? Who has ever dared to write that?

I remembered the fights in the ring and recalled the stress of medical school. Now there were no mistaken notions. It put the thoughts that things I had done were tough to get through in perspective. I was painfully reminded that so much in life is relative. The rags of one are the best clothes of another. A finely dressed couple gets out of a limo to attend a Broadway show while one hundred feet away, another human lies sleeping under newspaper and garbage.

I have no doubt I love my children deeply. They should be sure of that. Fatherhood without a helpmate was the toughest job I would ever have: This quest to finish what my wife and I had started. The task of raising them on my own. I had little desire left now to assume any more risk or confusion. Sure, the years to come would reveal my loneliness; a few girlfriends would come and go. It seemed unrealistic to think mixing families or trying to find someone to calm this storm would help, considering the massive mistake I had already made. Others surely had been successful in doing so, but unless God were to send someone special, my intent was to leave it alone.

I believed it was up to me to make this work. Not only to raise my children but to do it well enough that they would be stable, would contribute good things to the human race. I wanted them to be well adjusted even though I wasn't sure what that meant exactly. We had made the start, and it was a race I wasn't certain I could win or finish. But I had to give it my best.

I'd had little time to grieve. I am sure that didn't help me emotionally, but I would have to work it out somehow. For the time being, it was the children and me: the four of us, with the help of grandparents from time to time. It has come to me now that a universal truth in the agony of loss, since there is no changing it, is to move through it. Not that one ever really forgets or gets over it, as many might advise. Still, if you do not move through the pain, it will swallow you like sand and take the life you have left. It offers no quarter. One cannot shut it out, for it will surface somehow.

I think we are all called upon to face our fears head-on. Only when acceptance comes, and the willingness to walk through it, will the help and faith in a higher power be there to carry us when we feel faint, to help us not only survive but live above it, still able to smile and be a source of strength for others, which in turn brings courage for our own fight.

I drew a line in the sand. This would not be easy, but it was surely possible, and my duty was clear. I chose Texas, and it was as good as anywhere. My brother was there, and I thought we could repair our relationship. There might be some help for us both. There was for a time, but it didn't last.

The journey had begun, a time for which I couldn't prepare. Where were the classes for this? I don't know of a book today for perfect single parenting, a manual for all the possibilities. There are books that offer some ideas, but as far as I know, there is not one complete manual. I found none at the time for the single parent left to fight this fight and take the blows alone.

I had no one to work the corner. No cut man. No shouts of inspiration. No one to give a plan of attack. Every day I was fighting one round after another, just taking the punches and fighting back as best I could. That was the end of it. Fighting for survival. Breathing. Walking. One step at a time. That was all there was and all there is. Given the promise that love is the great healer of loss and pain, I withstood one day at a time. The truth in this is solid. A great deal of love is needed in these circumstances. But it was always running away— or was it? I was still standing. How could I without love? It was there even if I couldn't see it. It was the glue holding us together!

Wisdom dictates that a man should never be ashamed to admit he has been in the wrong—which is just saying he is wiser today than he was yesterday. The entire experience of Tamara's death and the aftermath was horrible. I remember once relaying to her that there was no need to be brokenhearted and broke. I had a million dollars of term life on me, should she be left alone. I had the reasoning to get a fraction of that on her life, so the kids and I might have a fighting chance for a new start should something happen to her. That would have been reality except for the house—the house we had waited so long to build—due to the builders' mistake. I paid the second mortgage with this death money. I auctioned the rest and let our nightmare become someone else's dream. The children and I left, both broke and brokenhearted—the very thing I had tried to avoid. I was angry with God, more than I knew at the time. It took years for me to accept part of the responsibility, the choices that had been mine. I lacked faith. In the end the results and consequences of some choices were mine. I hadn't caused all of this, and no doubt the misfortune was terrible. Yet I needed to own up to my part in it. If I desired, I could be angry with myself. I once heard a priest indicate he had learned one thing from life: there is a god, and it was not him. It was certainly not me either.

There are those who have traded in cards, attempting to gain better hands, only to go bust, making choices and decisions that helped something already tragic turn into an absurdity. Again I remind you that no matter what the problem is, you are not alone. If you are to survive, to live to fight another day—better yet, to live to love again—love will have to help you. You have the ability to forgive and love yourself despite the ignorance you may have shown. To err is human. After all, that is all we are here: human. Despite our limited exposure, we have not entered into a place of perfection and endless love. It should not be a surprise, then, that mistakes will be a part of us.

When you think of these things, show love to another. I have tried it. There are those whose stories are worse than mine. Whatever the case, when I give them love, my own regret and remorse seem to lessen. I walk away breathing a little more easily for the good I offered. You can as well.

Have you made mistakes? Certainly. Have you ever met anyone who claimed he or she had not? If you have, I advise you to consider walking away from them. These types of people can be rude and judgmental. At the least they are full of fear. There is no love in that. I have hope that my children watched me and learned. When trouble comes, make an effort to seek help and guidance of someone you trust if that is available. In some circumstances that may not be readily available, or sometimes people don't know what guidance to give. Should you have someone who can take that time, it can be very valuable—more than anything to have the time and resources to take time away from the daily grind, giving the mind a chance to recover, and having the advantage of clear wisdom and guidance and your own clarity to comprehend it. This does not indicate the heart is healed, for that may take years for some and a lifetime for others. Time does allow for us to live on and get better one day at a time. Emotional and psychological chaos combined with confusion and fear can and most often will lead to further self-destruction. Reach out to someone who can offer love and sound guidance at the time if available.

Try to remember not to wander into the darkness of your mind alone in the early-morning hours. Difficulty with insomnia and racing thoughts is not uncommon. During these times of pain and confusion, you are not in a safe place. It is far better to sit in the quiet with someone who can offer love and patience. He or she will be better equipped at the time to do the thinking for you until you're ready again. I certainly wish I had more of that at the time: help in keeping me out of my mind so that I might not have acted insane! In the darkness of the night after trauma, it is easy to recount mistakes and regrets. For those who feel, like I did, that there is no one to take over, I can only suggest calling out to God for his tender mercies: to fill your heart with love and to tame the beast inside the mind. Repeat the promises he has given over and over. Try to remember that God is love.

CHAPTER 12

CHILDREN
When strong foundations falter

All of the inspired things in this world were
born of love. It is our fear that taints them.
Darkness is not a thing or entity of
itself, only a lack of light. The absence of light
that creates darkness. Only a lack of love
creates fear. Fear is an idea we have created.
The real, substantial, only thing of truth is love.

—*Ali Faulkner*

W e started over in a small home close to an elementary school. That at least made sense. It was easy to walk the girls to school, and my son caught the bus to junior high. I had to get work that would allow the single-parenting efforts. Working nights at a hospital doing anesthesia as a way of making a living really wasn't possible now. I had experience treating pain. I could do this and control the hours and be there for the kids, so that was the direction I took. I dismissed the idea of returning to the military as the sole parent. I was uncertain of returning when it would readily be known that under the hardship I could not be deployed unless I turned the children over to grandparents to raise. Another choice. I was their father. I wanted to finish what their mother and I started.

I eventually took the specialty boards in pain, as I had in anesthesia. In time I was in practice. That was a blessing: being able to find a solution, a method of dealing with the madness of single parenting. During those years the children were, of course, young. I had many good times with them. It is amazing how God's grace abides over children. I knew within that they had to miss their mother. Like well-trained soldiers, they marched right on. They did well in school. Laughing and happy, they enjoyed our little home. We played games and had many a movie night. The girls shared a room with canopy beds—all white—and they looked like little princesses in their Cinderella room. My son and I were down the hall, across from each other. From the start I could keep an eye on him, and it didn't take long for me to see the reasons why I needed to. Tamara, before her death, had told me to watch him closely, for he would be the one to have trouble. To this day I don't know how she knew, but my God, she was correct. If I had known what was to come eventually, I probably would have raised a white flag and surrendered. Thank God for ignorance and not being able to see the difficulties to come when there had already been so much to bear.

We took some great vacations. I took the kids to Mexico. We went to Chicago and San Diego. I tried my hand at surfing. I became really good at dragging the ocean floor with my board and was thankful to survive without being bitten in half by a shark. I told the girls I was sorry, but we might just have to settle for bowling!

Those days ran by fast. Before I knew it, we were moving into a larger home, and junior high and high school were upon us. I did well in private practice before insurance changes, and we had a pool and many parties for the kids and their friends. How I wish I could go back and cook for them one more time.

Ali got involved in theater, and I had so many good times seeing her perform, especially in the lead roles she got in the high school musicals. I realize now these were the best of days. There were times, though, when I lay awake thinking of Tamara. Why had I been left to see these things without her? I cried more than once over this. I needed her, but only through faith could I have the notion that somehow she was there. Ali had her mother's voice, and it echoed across the theater. I could hear Ali and her mother at the same time. Such a blessing.

Gentry became a track star, and with her wins and her top-ten times in the mile in the state, I believed she was destined to win a state medal. But she was pushed too hard.

Gentry always ran both the mile and two-mile. I talked to her coach and her and asked that they pick one or the other. I guess he disagreed, for she kept running both. Then it happened. She collapsed with a bad case of mono. That ended the running for quite a while. She eventually ran again and finished well but never was the same. That is a hard virus to overcome. We all enjoyed watching her, shouting and cheering her on. She was a tough one and hard to beat. How I miss those days. She recently sent me an article from California. She came in second place in a marathon. When I saw her running time, I knew after all these years she was finally back: the gazelle again. I think that was the best time for distance she ever had.

Taylor began his troubles in high school: A couple of fights. Alternative school. A young man in trouble. I could only think maybe there was a connection between Tamara's death and him being our oldest child. I had run a boxing gym for troubled kids in Missouri but was forced to quit when Tamara became ill. Taylor never got to finish boxing the way he wanted. He had won many fights and trophies. It made sense to me when he came and asked if I would train him for the Golden Gloves in Fort Worth. He was older, and he wanted to win to prove he still had it. I thought it might help him get through his troubles. We did it: Trained hard. Found a gym so he could spar. Hit the bag. Punched the mitts. Had a couple of warm-up fights prior to the contest.

When the fight came, I felt he was ready. It was a tough, hard fight. After the second round, it seemed about even to me. So in the corner, I said, "Son, meet him in the middle of the ring, and throw everything you've got. Don't stop till you hear the bell." I had bought a card for him before the fight. On it was a kitten looking into a mirror and seeing a great lion. After wiping him down and giving him water, I repeated the instructions. When he stood up, I showed him the card. His eyes lit up. I asked him to see the lion.

In the end, it was enough. He won. His grandpa and best friend were there, and, of course, his sisters. It was a good night for him. I was very proud of him, and some of my friends came as well. I hoped that would be the end of trouble for him. God knows I wish that were the truth. It wasn't. I have read books about words, about how powerful they are. What should be spoken and what should not? Were his mother's words to me on her deathbed a curse? I know how strong and full of faith she was when she died. I am confident her words were not a curse, only a warning from a mother with instinct.

My son and I have spoken about this. We have together accepted the belief that neither of us is cursed. People get confused. They get hurt. Sometimes we make poor choices. I couldn't say much about the fighting, even when he beat a few other guys senseless one night. I had done the same in my youth after my mother's suicide. The property damage to another's vehicle? Anything less than a thousand was a misdemeanor. Over that, a felony. The damage was just enough. With only three months to go for a previous offense, he violated his probation. That resulted in more trouble.

This chapter is for parents, for those who have experienced a troubled child. I share it for their pondering. I wish to let all of you understand you are not alone in this heartbreak and pain.

It is not my intention to embarrass my son or make him feel bad. None among us is perfect, and God knows that without mercy I have no chance for peace in eternity. I am quite sure if Taylor knew the pain he was going to cause over a decade to those he loved, he would not have done what he did. For sure he wouldn't have wanted to pay his own price for those moments of insanity.

I don't see the need to go into great detail—only enough to reflect on the magnitude of these indiscretions and the cost incurred. I will summarize by saying that despite his college degree, it was a matter of time before the trouble with the law began. Nothing I could do seemed able to stop this. The amount of pain that a disobedient child can inflict upon a parent is immeasurable.

The time came when I endured visiting my son through glass, by the phone the prison provided. Every time I left, I would go to the car and weep with agony. There were times I had to wait for fifteen minutes before I could drive home. The tears were not only for him but for me as well. I felt I had failed him somehow.

My promise to Tamara had not been in vain, however. Through the years I fought to keep him alive, never abandoning him to fight alone.

Finally, he was released, and when that day came, my soul jumped. My heart finally beat with a steady rhythm again. It was not to last, though, and over time more trouble came. When drugs and bad peer influences take hold, it seems impossible to wrench the ones we love from the vise of trouble and possible death. It was a long ten-year battle, but finally it appears to be over. He lived through it by God's grace and my CPR, given to him while waiting for an ambulance. I don't know how I lived through it, honestly. I am confident it was by God's grace and mercy. Not everyone survives this battle for life. I am very proud of my son for doing so!

There was a short time when Taylor considered turning pro as a fighter. But he was finished by a knee injury requiring significant surgery. I don't think his heart was in it regardless. Taylor lost the will to fight, at least to inflict any physical pain on anyone. I understood that. I remain convinced there was a time he could have been champ. But he has won a far greater battle at present.

He found himself in sound engineering school in California. He currently is writing music and is working full time. His sisters have offered much support. My daughter's husband pushes Taylor forward and encourages him all he can. Thank you, Bobby, for your love. At present Taylor is doing well. He made the choice to get help rather than fight without a trainer—the choice to live and do it abundantly, to its fullest and without any regret. He is a better person for all of it, the good and bad. He's living close to Ali and Bobby during this rebuilding phase. Ali is continuing with her acting career and public speaking, among other endeavors. Gentry is a registered nurse.

In our family Gentry is known as the rock. It is not easy to move her off a path she has chosen. That is obvious from what I wrote above. I credit her for being a source of inspiration to Taylor, along with help from her sister, Ali. It was Ali who, at a critical point, called me and asked we not surrender hope regarding their brother and my son.

It was suggested I try a form of love called tough love. This type of love is hard to give. I never became very good with this so-called tough love. I did make an effort once. I learned, however, that once legal issues develop, it isn't easy to get a second chance. For those without love and support, including forgiveness, there can be the temptation to repeat illegal activity to survive. I think our justice system fails in this regard. In short, this was not a time when tough love would have made anything better, in my opinion. I talked to someone who gave tough love a try as well. In this person's case, a phone call came from a sibling in trouble, and he ignored it. His brother died after the call. Sometimes rock bottom is death. I considered that when hanging on for my son's life. My son is presently a stronger and better person than I can ever recall him being. He is sober. He made that choice. No doubt he can use all the help he can get. The fight will be from day to day. There is nothing he wouldn't do to help someone else. He and I have shared many tears together. He was incredibly filled with regret. That is over, for there is no love in it. He is assured that love commands he move forward focused on the positives.

People generally pay their debts for wrongdoing. It can take quite an effort for the law to let go. Taylor's offenses caused no permanent damage, no loss of limb or life. In my opinion, there was no need to carry a mark for life, no reason to lose the rights of a citizen. I think that is a mistake unless it is a capital crime and life has been taken. One has to consider the continued risk to others, weighing the individual circumstances with mercy and forgiveness as well as law and justice. I certainly think there are things that can happen that people should pay for, but there are minor crimes for which second chances shouldn't be quite so hard to get. All I can offer in advice is that after I am gone, my son will continue to live righteously and without further regret. Only love.

The Texas house and the kids who were in it are gone—gone their own ways. I ended up by myself, so fatigued that I cared not to keep the place and take care of it. More than once I have felt that I should have kept a home for the certainty or security it would offer, however false pretense that would be. After all, we leave everything behind for the children to deal with anyway.

The nights alone with only my rescued dogs in the one-bedroom loft I now call home are very different from what was. There won't be a lot for the children to deal with. After all I have endured, whatever I decide to do should remain simple. I understand the desire to accumulate things. Things are pleasant to look at. Things can command a certain amount of status in this world—status that appears to attract love, when in reality things simply don't. They can attract a form of love, but generally not a healthy one.

Whenever I see the children, I force back tears. I always take the opportunity to hold them close to me, wishing it could last forever. Having faith gives hope that after this life, in eternity we will never have to be apart. I feel pride that they are all alive and doing well. Gentry is in love and married to a navy pilot. Ali works in movies and public speaking, and she is also married to a wonderful young man. I see their courage as they navigate from Dallas to LA, allowing her to pursue her dreams.

Taylor is alive, believing he has a future and holding steady. He has renewed hope, combining his finance degree with sound engineering and athletic training certification. The expungements for petty crimes have begun. I indicate this to all parents and young men and women who have endured or been involved in such matters. It doesn't take much wrong to undue and ruin a right. I would far rather be judged by a God rather than a man or woman. I pray my children don't place too much importance on things. I did for a short time. It seems that despite my weakness regarding things early on, they all have a grip on that. I certainly got over whatever desire I had for things!

Long gone are the days of the little ones next to me while we played games or watched movies. So too are the days of watching them grow, with the track meets and theater performances. So too is that night Taylor stood in the center of the ring and, like so many times before, refused to go down but instead stood toe to toe with his adversary. My prayer is that every day from this point on, he will stand toe to toe and never surrender again in a fight much harder to win than a boxing match. For the single parent and all those who have suffered long, sleepless nights, all of you who have cried out in agony, as given in the example of sacrifice on the cross between father and son, I feel your pain. I understand.

Once children come into your life, it is never again your own. To the end of life, you never ever again belong to your own selfish desires—that is, of course, if you care. There are only memories filled with the faces and souls, whether happy or tormented, that you and a mate brought into this world. This chapter, of course, will remain unfinished and continue after I have joined their mother.

For those brave ones who had no idea what they were doing at the time they brought life into a place where death is required, I salute you. I have listened to many patients tell me about the problems and pain family and children have brought them. Everyone has his or her own story to tell.

Emotional pain combined with physically debilitating conditions are hard to live with. I certainly have dealt with both many times. Each time I have listened about the pain and the scars of war. If victory comes, it is, again, with the help of this powerful emotion called love. Whether referred to as tough or not, it is still love. Always love. I remember something I read once. I leave this with my son: "A great man is what he is because he was what he was."

One of my children told me that during their raising, despite my love, at times I could be harsh. I didn't like hearing that at first. I became defensive and hurt. After careful reflection I knew it was most likely true in some way. It was difficult to do everything on my own, and at times fatigue and the tremendous responsibility pressured me, especially when one of my children went down the wrong path. I had no one to bounce things off of. All I could tell them was that I had done my best. Although the circumstances were harsh from time to time, I do believe a tremendous amount of love was there. There was no argument regarding that. Still, one does the best he can, and my greatest defense is that single parenting was simply the hardest duty I ever had. Until my death I don't think the children will fully realize what I sacrificed for them—the choices I might have made should I have never had them, for example. In many ways I hope they don't have to. That would mean they also would have to experience it. Frankly, I wouldn't wish it on anyone, much less them. To the extent they do, it will help them to understand what true unconditional love is.

For those of you who have lost a child, I cannot understand your pain, though I have come close with my son. I pray I never do, that God allows me to go first. That's more natural than selfish, I would think. Let me assure you of this again: you are not alone. There are others who feel your pain. Yet you can have the hope that only love can give. There is a day coming when love will allow you to see, touch, and feel your child again. Life being a test, we must endure for reasons unknown, but how great the moment when the certainty of uncertainty is finally resolved, the moment when those you loved so deeply are returned by the love lost. This time love will remain. This time you will not ever lose it again. Accepting and believing this may not be easy for everyone. It was and at times still is a struggle for me. I can with confidence express this thought to you: if you choose not to believe in a life after this one, your life will likely become tiresome, full of fatigue. You'll appear better off dead than alive. One way will lead you to fear, death, and regret. The other will help you be ready and prepared to live and die well. You and I can do this. We should.

I was very inspired by something my daughter Ali shared: "There is no healing by taking a bat and beating darkness over the head with it. Only love can heal. That starts with self-love. Unconditional and pure, radiating outward."

My son let me know he was finally understanding how important self-esteem is, how vital it is in believing one can do anything. A friend shared with him, "If you want to build self-esteem, do esteemed things."

Gentry told me once it was hard to always know the right thing to do. "Maybe there wasn't right or wrong," she said. "We simply do, and maybe that is right enough!" My children have told me they wouldn't rather have had another dad. I no doubt feel the same about them as my children, despite the troubles regarding my son. They indicated I had done more than enough regarding love and devotion. Thoughts like these, expressed by my children, let me consider the possibility that I had not failed. Love will grant me a passing grade. It will for you as well. All who have loved and sacrificed for their children understand. There is constant chatter, and we must struggle to shut down worry regarding our children in a hard world. Did we do enough? Did we do too much? Shut up, mind. Enough! We did our best. When we love deeply, it helps to create the should, would, or could. Why? Do we really expect perfection? That is not possible. We must choose to accept our best.

I asked my son to please consider his choices, not only for himself but for his family. When a child doesn't do well, it seems to stick with a parent. I think it's true that there can be cause and effect. Some children turn out better than they should have considering the lack of instruction and love. Others have issues they brought on themselves despite the advantages they were given. I am confident that many parents have been blessed or blamed unfairly. Again, love would ask that a parent and child forgive themselves and each other for poor choices and inevitable mistakes.

I share these thoughts with you. I believe it best to let go with peace, knowing we did our best, to once again let love be the judge while moving ever forward in our journey home. Let love be the guiding light and the hope of renewed energy. I repeat that I personally have woken up at the 3:00 a.m. hour and suffocated in the "should have" or "could have" dilemma and chaos. Again, the rearview mirror is small. The front window is much larger, with more possibilities. This calls upon us to look ever ahead and move forward. We do not gain ground by forever backing up. Be still. Let yourself understand that if you loved to the best of your ability, you did all you could. Let love be enough!

CHAPTER 13

RELATIONSHIPS
Tough love

Love always brings difficulties, that is true,
but the good side of it is that it gives energy.

—*Vincent Van Gogh*

I think it is hard and complicated to move into another relationship when one has already had a good or bad one. The memories are there, and in time they do fade or heal, as the case may be. Yet, though it's not fair, there is the comparison, the expectation that if I had this before, why should I settle for less or not have more? This makes it difficult on both parties, because one is convinced this is not as good as what was lost and the other tries to make up for the relationship that failed miserably. This is not always the case. Sometimes people just can't find favor in one another. There are those who have many failed relationships for good reason. The fact is that we as humans tend to be selfish. God bless those who have had the pleasure of having fifty or more years together.

Despite the above, I attempted to date, from forty-three to sixty-three. Some came from friends who introduced me to someone, others from dating sites online. Only once or twice up to the present did I come close to a second chance after my tremendous loss. To this day I cannot fully understand why there was failure in two cases. I accept responsibility for my portion in these matters, especially one of them. She changed after her mother died. During that event I somehow offended her. People have a right to grieve in the way they see fit. I certainly should have understood that. I think after a time, she came to the realization that she didn't love me, at least not enough to enter into a marriage of souls. It hurt at the time. But she did us both a big favor. Naturally, this being the case, our relationship would have failed.

The other was a case of temperament. After my experience of the loss of my wife, I wasn't able to tolerate much when it came to arguing. I needed someone who would remain relatively mild mannered. My emotional status was unable to handle anything else. I recall purchasing a $300 necklace for this girlfriend's birthday.

She informed me she felt it was too cheap a gift. I never felt the same toward her after that. She gave it back, and I in turn gave it to one of my daughters. Everything in life is relative.

Mixing families when each has children is not easy. Being with someone who has no kids of his or her own would be fine if that person always wanted children but couldn't have them. However, when it is someone who never wanted them at all, how can that work?

I had no other thing that was more important than my devotion to my children. To be in a contest between them and another was a failure waiting to happen. One woman I was dating told me, "Listen! You are doing too much for your son. I want you to stop if you expect us to be together." It was of interest when one of her children called me and didn't have good things to say about the current relationship with her mother. Regardless, I never had anything to say about how she dealt with her children. I didn't believe I had earned the right. After all, we were not married. I couldn't turn my back on my son. I elected instead to turn away from her. Right or wrong, regarding my son, I never regretted that choice. For me there never was a choice.

I always believed that in the majority of these efforts, I was a giver. I have been and still am today. Two givers should work. A giver and a taker will eventually fail, in my opinion. Takers are never satisfied. They continually look for more. Finally, the givers understand the takers will never stop. The givers, now enlightened, become exhausted. They end the pain and give up on giving. They simply give out. In some cultures, after the death of a mate, there is never any effort made to start over. I understand this now despite the loneliness.

It may make some sense to wait until all children are on their own (for the most part) before trying to move on in life with another partner. The disadvantage is that no one gets any younger. Time marches on, and the choices are not as numerous. Some get more attractive with age, like fine wine. Sadly, most don't. The crude fact is that unless we make efforts to take care of ourselves, increasing age is generally not attractive. For most, youth and having little money go hand in hand. It is generally expected. Even if you maintain a good income for your later years, it is still not an assurance that you won't be living alone, but I can think of worse things than living alone—like living with someone without love and wishing to be alone!

At the end of the day, at least there is the discovery that this issue is not as easy as one might think. Nothing much ever is. One thing I do know for certain: with my upbringing, I needed someone with an even temperament. There was no way I could navigate through anything less.

I am thankful for good times in relationships that eased the pain, even if it was for only a little while. Bowling or going to a movie instead of spending time alone. The meals we shared. Those who did take an interest in my children or even offered advice. There were a few I met who, without a doubt, I wished I hadn't. I learned from them, so it wasn't a waste. After the fact, though, I did have to ask, Was that really necessary? The sad truth is that some along the way surely felt this way about me. A sobering thought.

I recall the time I was invited over to a date's apartment after dinner. She wanted to show me her collection of knives. I thought that was a little unusual for a woman but different and interesting. That was until I saw where they were displayed. Nearly fifty hung on her bedroom walls. I decided not to stay the night. I remember being glad to be home.

I have never been much of a smoker, but I understand why some people do it, even after realizing it doesn't usually end well. Once when I was out on a date, the woman asked me to stop and get some smokes. My thought was that I should be giving and do it. When she returned to the car with a couple of cartons (because they were on sale), that wasn't a good sign. My God! She smoked so much, I thought she would turn into an ashtray before the night was over. Taking a break from the dance floor, and with her in the restroom, I lit up six cigarettes and placed them in my mouth. All of them! When she returned she asked, "What are you doing?" I told her I was trying to catch up. There was not much of an attempt for a kiss good night.

Another one I find hard for anyone to top is the woman who had a problem keeping her clothes on in public. I understand there are strippers, and they get paid for such. I don't judge them. Only God knows what they have been through. Men pay to see it, so we are as much to blame, if there is fault. I did this myself once or twice on an invite, with the declaration it would somehow help me. It didn't. Just another moment to be ashamed of. I spent most of the time conversing with the women, asking them why they were doing such a thing. A stupid question. Of course it was for the money and to entertain some idiot like me while I was there. I naturally left thinking I needed to save someone from this kind of life. Here is a thought to live with: don't try to save someone who didn't ask for help.

This was different, though. When this woman had a little too much to drink, she simply took her blouse and bra off—in the restaurant! After being asked to leave, and with the police on their way, I processed intellectually that having dinner with this person was not worth it. Of interest is that this person could be and was at times very decent and helpful. Looking back, I believe it was simply a bad combination—her and the alcohol, that is. Maybe there was some reaction with prescribed drugs. Perhaps a bipolar disorder untreated. Most find this account difficult to believe, but I am not a liar.

Of course, it is pleasant to have dinner and, upon leaving the place, meet your date's spouse in the parking lot, not knowing, of course, that the marriage was still intact. Not much to say in this situation. There is the other party's belief you are lying about not knowing. It most often comes down to presenting the offer to walk away or fight. Thank God the fight didn't happen in that case.

In one case, I did care for the woman but couldn't understand her father. He was wealthy, and it became obvious he was not very tolerant of a man coming along to ride on the skirts of his wealth, which would eventually be hers. To this day I believe I would have ruined her inheritance. If he had cut her off, I never could have replaced it. The only way I could prove to him it wasn't about the money was to leave. He may have liked me after that. Some in his family made fun of my background, the lack of money. I didn't respect that. They considered my background uncultured. There came a time when I would have been more than happy to show just how uncivilized I could be. Then again, what would this have to do with love?

The last example of love gone strange is somewhat embarrassing. I won't spend much time on it. All I can say is that when someone brings a suitcase full of special toys and begins to explain why they must be used to have pleasure, the choice is clear. Have an endless supply of batteries or frankly pass? I passed.

Why did I share these things? I wanted to indicate that each of us has experiences in the fight to find love in the form of healthy relationships. We are all guilty of being selfish at times. I want to acknowledge that blame doesn't always rest with you and me. Others have their issues as well. Because of this we can easily start finding fault with others and find every excuse to cast the fault or failure on them. The simple truth is that I was an ass at times. I think I drank more often during that time. Love taught me to stop this. Love was telling me to understand all fault was not mine, yet I was far from innocent.

One thing I became very guilty of: I had learned to be afraid that love would fail me. Because of this I took every opportunity to run away. There came a time when I could easily find multiple excuses to run. Certainly this helped me to avoid pain. It also negated chances to love again and is the principal reason I am alone today. Yet as I have noted, love helped me to understand that even though I currently don't look up and see anyone, love is present. I am not alone. Love remains.

My first fights were in grade school and junior high. I was picked on because of my small size. Years of wrestling and boxing, with a fair amount of weightlifting and maturity, eventually helped. I wasn't usually thought of as easy prey, so I escaped most conflicts. As a young man, when I was attacked by a larger man (I referred to this earlier), in self-defense I nearly beat him to death. I never forgot it. It happened outside a shopping mall. He tried to run over a crowd of people, including me, my date, and another couple as we were leaving a theater.

His car skidded to a stop. The girl I was with asked him if he was crazy. That was enough to get her threatened.

I tried to intervene. Before I knew it, I was on the ground, dropped like a bag of potatoes. He was choking me. I thought this was the end. I don't remember much after that. I know what I was told: that I came off the ground and hit him with a barrage of punches that moved him back to his car. I dragged him like a paper sack. It ended with several people pulling me off him while I was smashing his head into the trunk of his car. On the way home, holding an ice bag over my eye, I became frightened. I realized things like this could end negatively no matter who was to blame. A life could be changed forever. It's not worth it unless there is simply no choice, when life is threatened. I was told I informed him I hoped his soul was God's, since his ass was mine. We left him by his car. Looking back, I saw him slowly getting up, so he had to be OK. It was self-defense, but those with me told me it was best to leave.

I mentioned my outcomes when it came to dating. I did have a couple of girlfriends who were good, as I stated. They did a lot for the kids and me. I did a lot for them in return. These were the few close calls I referred to. I thought about the possibility of marriage, the idea of trying again. As I said, I may never know why at least one of them didn't work out. Maybe I didn't give enough soon enough or didn't believe they loved me. It was hard to think I was settling for less than what I'd had or tempting them to do the same. Perhaps no one was to blame. Reasons may sometimes never be completely understood. One thing is true: our ability to truly love failed at some point.

Who really desires to be with someone who doesn't love him or her deeply? Some do this and spend their lives doing everything they can to gain others' love. In a few cases, it has worked. I have listened to many tell me it never did.

Eventually I even subjected myself to a foreign spouse-finding scam. As most advise, never send money! When I recall this desperate act, I know it was about revenge toward other women who had treated me disrespectfully. I wanted to say, look at this: you treated me this way, and look what I have now, and all she needed was a green card! It was fitting that I was the one who got taken. Money was sent but no one showed up. Loneliness and the fear of being alone are powerful emotions. These emotions are responsible for poor choices. This powerful emotion created within me a lack of sound judgment. I had no confidant.

At times I turned to the children. I have later in life understood this also can be a mistake. Children who love us want us to be happy but do not care to listen to the negatives regarding relationships, if for no other reason than it serves as a reminder that their mother is gone. Without her these events occurred. With her they would not have. Women are different in this regard.

Women talk to other women. They are able to go to a sister. I did not have that and in general men don't tend to cultivate relationships outside of family. Most often a man will confide in his wife. Without her my tendency was to develop a codependency on the children. This is not healthy. It can result in a parent being looked at as less than an independent figure. In fact children are expected to come to us with their troubles, not so much the contrary.

I am confident there are favorable outcomes regarding different efforts like mine in relationship hunting. Two people from different cultures can find love. More often than not, citizenship and money are the priority. Despite multiple and different kinds of attempts, another meaningful relationship didn't work out for me.

Few are interested in restrictions when it comes to money. I have learned that enjoying money with travel and fine dining is not a mortal sin. Nor are vacations with those you love. Family. However, when it comes to mating, to be charitable and look to help those less fortunate while expecting love in return, I believe, is being a fool for love—an idiot, I suppose.

I got so lonely at one point I hired an escort for dinner and conversation. Just to talk. Nothing past that. Perhaps an embrace. Maybe she had done more with others. I was an easy mark. Why would she do anything she didn't have to? Thank God. For in reality, that is flirting with what could be illegal activity. Some in this sort of business actually hate the opposite sex. At least it would seem so by their words and actions. As stated one can get very lonely—not a good time to consume alcohol. Loneliness and lack of restraint will cloud good judgment. It is hard to feel the arrows of loneliness. It is best to utilize sober judgment.

I finally got over all the searching within myself and not feeling the presence of a higher power. This is self-inflicted torture and pain. The results are not good in most if not all cases. There was a time when a much younger woman approached me at a restaurant and gave me her number. I really couldn't understand why. I asked, and she indicated age was only a number. I did go to dinner with her, and it was flattering, an ego boost. I suppose famous and wealthy people have this happen all the time. That's not the case for me. I did have a wonderful dinner in large part because it reminded me of Tamara, when youth and love were more in the present and not the past. I didn't see the younger woman for quite some time after that; however, I did get a call later. She was in trouble and needed money for what she said was rent and books for school. I met her at a gas station and gave it to her. I encouraged her to try to do better and not settle for less than the best she could think of. That was the last time I ever saw her. I hope she listened. I think it was an effort on my part to make up for mistakes I had made, an effort to be good and giving. There was nothing physical between us, and I am glad for that. I doubt there could have been, with me thinking of the ages of my own daughters. The reality was that although she counted the age difference out, in the end it was there. We both knew it. She kept my number, though not for another date—only in case she was in financial need.

I think that is enough. There's no point in recalling further events or why relationships failed. I do want to use this opportunity to apologize to anyone I offended along the way. I think the point is that despite prayer and petition to God for another chance, they don't always come easily. There are always lessons learned and opportunities for growth. With reflection, one can argue the prayers to God should change. Be thankful for the good things you have had, and don't be too quick to ask for more. What one can get from this is a lesson in wisdom. Pray, as did Solomon, for wisdom to guide you in the process. Many times we overlook the fine print in the warranty. Be gracious and content that what you might think is in your best interest is not necessarily so.

For those of you who have lost love and found it again, be very thankful. You are extremely blessed. For those who looked and became frightful by what you found, I understand. It's better in some cases to shut the door behind you than be locked inside, looking for a window to jump out of!

For two years, I did not date at all. I had given up on myself. I'm older now—wiser, I think—and in many ways have something to offer. At other times, considering financial setbacks, I don't feel I have anything. This world looks at things. I mean *things*! What do you have or not, materially? Your success or failure is based on this.

I took chances. I took risks. I lived with tragedies. I have excuses and reasons not to be materially wealthy. I came close to being worth a few million on at least one if not two occasions. I got involved in what turned out to be a bad real estate investment at the wrong time. Anyone else remember 2008? A friend encouraged me to buy property he and another were partnering on. They backed out, and I was left to go on or fail to close. I decided I could hold and make some profit. Everything bottomed out, including the insurance payments of my medical practice. Another poor choice—or bad timing, depending on how one looks at it. Today the same property that was to hold my office practice and others has a small hospital sitting on it. It did sell for three times what I paid for it.

After everything has been considered, how sad it is to look at myself and not think I would be a blessing to most anyone's life. Is it humility? Is it shame? Is it the fatigue of having tried too hard for too long? What happens to us in this life to beat us? The truth is, at this point, considering all I have disclosed, I don't believe I have much to offer. No doubt there is no love in this manner of thought. Not at all. No matter what happens now, or not, I will not continue with that type of thinking. Love commands different. The fact is I do have love to offer!

In boxing I trained on a heavy bag that at first was like concrete, hard enough to break a hand if I wasn't careful. By the time I was through with it, the bag had softened up a lot. It was more user friendly. I think pain in life can soften us. It can humble us and remove pride that has no place in love at all. This is a good thing. Yet if we are not careful and let the punches take too heavy a toll, we become the bag: a shell of what we were, no more than a hanging bag.

I think this is in truth a lack of faith. Even the complete loss of it. With faith comes hope and belief. Gratitude and blessing. Regaining that is life itself: knowing there is something else, something beyond the pain.

Eternal love. That will bring peace and value again. Regarding this, I do have something to offer! Not money, though. Relative to others in this world, I am monetarily wealthy. Quite ironic. I am content that I steadily work on regaining faith and strength. This is belief in living beyond poor choices, an attempt not to let regret win.

It was said in a Western movie I love, "I already have the guilt. Might as well have the money!" Ideally, though, surely it is much better not to carry the guilt. Offer in truth love. Love is the greatest gift. Some do prefer money. Maybe most. It is needed. One can't pay the rent without it. It's hard to beg for food. Once the basics are covered, all the rest is gravy and overrated. The excess of it can ruin love. The greatest gift is love, and how grievous to make a mockery out of it. It has been said few things are sourer than one's own bitterness. This poison does more damage than most any other negative. You are the victim of yourself.

There may be some reading this who will judge. I am laying out my life as an example. Perhaps some who know me will choose never to speak to me again. At least there is no hypocrisy here, no vanity left. There is either mercy and forgiveness or judgment. I would rather be judged by God than another human. All I can do is again ask for forgiveness for anyone I've offended along the way. I hope love will allow you to forgive.

Not all relationships are of the dating nature. There are friendships and even family to consider. I have some good friends. It is said no greater love does a person have than to lay down his or her life for a friend. This has happened countless times in war. But I doubt there are many justifiable reasons to ask something this extreme when considering everyday life. As my dad said, "To be able to count true friends on one hand before death is to be blessed." I think he was referring to friends who would help even when the circumstances were not comfortable for them. On the other hand, one should consider how far he or she would go in asking a favor. If you were a true friend, you might not desire to place your friendship under more strain than is reasonable. I have experienced this and reasoned that the relationship had no love in it. Attempts to explain this to the other party failed. I had to leave him alone, with the hope that someday he might choose to love others as much as he did himself.

I maintain that even love allows for the preserving of one's sanity. Someone may ask another for more than he or she can possibly give. The sadness comes when the so-called friend is offended when you let him or her know you don't have it to give. That is different from promising to do something and then backing out. Worse yet is leading someone to do something that causes trouble.

There are people who have determined they are never wrong or unjust. They cannot make mistakes, and there is no need for them to apologize to anyone. Also, they have no limits on what they will ask you to do. This is very disturbing to me, and, quite frankly, it calls into question the idea that they are friends at all. It can become difficult and so confusing that one is forced to make difficult decisions. For example, there came a time when a friend would ask me for favors that were simply too costly for me. No matter how many I honored, another request would come. There was no consideration for what I had endured in my life or the needs of my family, only the narcissistic view that I had betrayed or been disloyal. The requests made of me were not pleas for food or necessities. The requests were not sound and made no sense. They were selfish and unnecessary.

I think in some cases, people like this would demand your very soul. There is no love in this. Self-indulgent people set no limits or boundaries. Even after one has battled in their favor on more than one occasion, another fight comes. There is no end. The so-called friendship takes emotional, psychological, and financial tolls. This can attack one's health, and the reality soon comes that feeding this self-centeredness has to stop. I think love in these circumstances does allow for walking away. After all, there is one who died on the cross for us who was innocent. None of us are capable of that. I have reasoned that crucifixion is not necessary to prove love unless a life is at stake.

It's better to move away from this type of relationship before love is replaced with the ugliness of bitterness or even hatred. I do believe love in its true form is giving to one another gracefully and not taking from someone selfishly. To love is to be loved and give love. Love has nothing to do with taking from another. It is a gift and is given freely. Love is not demanding. All one can do is love and forgive but then move away from the relationship upon realizing the love given is not being returned but is instead replaced with the nonproductive need to ask for things that make no sense. This is a different form of loving: Loving but not liking. Forgiving but not continuing. Perhaps this is an example of what has been thought of as *tough love.*

I have accepted I may live out the rest of my life alone. I have indicated that love can free us of that belief. I suppose it is fitting. There are the children, God, a few close friends. I don't expect to love a woman again, neither to give it or receive it. In truth, I may not expect it. Within myself I have a feeling love from another could come. I believe I could give a lot, as I have in the past. I have had chances come and go. I am not young physically any longer. I've chosen poorly. However, I feel young at times, and certainly wiser.

One thing is certain: in the process, I have gotten over myself. It took far too long, but I am thankful it finally happened. The last time I tried to date, when asked about myself, I was far too tired to render an answer. All I could think was, *Soon there will be a book. Read that.*

Love would ask far more of me. It does of you as well. It would dictate not to give up on myself, for there is no love in that! Why am I sharing the negativity? For one solid reason: that you will know for certain that others share the thoughts you have—others like me.

I was reminded of the idea of getting over oneself recently while shopping. A store employee asked if she might help me. I responded, "I hope so."

"What are you looking for?" she asked.

"What do you have?" I said.

"We have slacks, jackets, and pants on sale."

"That is what I will have," I said.

"Any particular colors?" she continued.

"No. Any color will do."

A quick and no-nonsense sale, for sure. She commented she'd had fun and wished everyone were that easy. I replied, "No worries. I am over myself." I left wondering if she understood.

If I remain alone in the physical realm, it is for reasons, if for no other than the conflict within myself. When you lose faith during the fight for sanity, living can simply get the best of you. Waking up to realize you are lost allows you to feel that you have nothing to offer yourself, much less another. Most women desire security, stability, strength. I had those for a time. The trials weakened me. Out of grief I gained resolve, only to be beaten on again. I do understand how hard it can be to hold on. There can be a blessing from what seems to be a curse. You realize that outside of a connection with a higher power, there is a certain void. In the end, if we submit to and lean upon that power, then through resolve we finish strong and go out loving despite ourselves. Thankfully, I am stronger.

If I have struck a chord in this chapter, I hope it is this: if you have found love after losing it, I am very proud of you and your ability to love again. At some point, to succeed you had to love. Love yourself again, and love another. You have tapped in to the power of what love can do for those like me, living alone due to the various reasons I have explored. What shall we do? If we yet have time, we will have to forgive ourselves as well as others. We will have to love ourselves again. In loving, the love of others may again find us, for love attracts love. Being insecure and feeling that we are forever lost and without anything meaningful to offer is not love. Love is and forever will be the final eraser, the mathematics that solve the equation.

At sixty-three, am I done? Done with love from a romantic side? Perhaps I am. Let it not be from a lack of love within myself. If I go, let me go out loving. Let that be my and your history. May what we recall about our lives and experiences here be remembered with love: That which we gave. That which we received. It can be sobering and very lonely to realize there were too many lovers and not enough love.

I have discussed with many the pain and anguish brought about by failed relationships and divorce. Second only to untimely and tragic death, this emotional devastation of failed love offers suffering and pain that can last for decades. This only reaffirms how important love is, for the lack of it is agonizing! Only the return of love will negate the loss of it!

CHAPTER 14

BANKRUPTCY
The measure of wealth

Love never claims, it ever gives.
Love never suffers, never resents,
never revenges itself.

—Gandhi

As I have noted, I was never able to recommend medical school to my children. The truth is, I felt it was a very hard road full of holes. This may happen to others in different professions. It would not be surprising to me if actors, teachers, police officers, and many other workers in other trades and professions have done the same with their children. My belief is there was a time in this country when job satisfaction was higher, such as after the Great Depression and during the time of the Industrial Revolution. Before the inflation of the 1980s seemed to be a decent time in history for many in this nation. It was fairly easy for most to make decent livings and pay cash for homes and cars. Homes appreciated in value. There were no credit cards. Pensions existed more often than not.

I certainly understand there was a time when the commitment given to become a physician was considered worth it financially, for the monetary return was great when compared to the majority of other professions or careers. Then came managed care. I argue medicine is about the best example of a sector of the capitalist society that has been driven to a socialistic state. Before I go further, this is not about pity or an attempt to make others feel sorry for physicians. Rather, it is about understanding, about being educated concerning the process. I have alluded to this previously and have spoken about the gift of healing, the satisfaction gained from that, and why I believe it is necessary to place value in such matters to be satisfied in the medical profession. There are still those who found ways to adapt and make large sums of money. Certain specialists are able to run their businesses with cash payments, such as cosmetic surgeons. I would like to address the quest for the American dream and what can happen when the rules are changed.

I started premed at eighteen, worked my way through my undergrad years, and enlisted in the military. Afterward I returned to school and invested four years in medical school followed by four years in post-graduate training. I never made much money during these years and graduated from the experience at the age of thirty-four. For me, then, it was a sacrifice of youth. The experience wasn't over, though, because I incurred massive school debt. I've touched on this, but I feel the need to repeat it. This debt took four years to pay off, as my wife and I gave our full attention to it. We knew if we didn't, it would never be paid. Some of the interest wasn't deferred, as some of the loans came from outside the government. The fact is, I paid back the better part of $170,000. I borrowed half of that to pay for tuition and living while in school, but it doubled before I could pay it back.

I was then thirty-eight, and for the first time in my life, I was making money as a doctor without owing anything. To me that was a little late, and, combined with the reduced salaries of the young physicians in the '90s versus those of a decade or two prior, factoring in cost of living, I had my doubts this had been worth it financially for me as an individual. Despite that, I went forward, viewing it as a calling, and set about trying to help patients who were less fortunate.

We experienced only two years of financial freedom before my wife became terminally ill. As I mentioned, this added more fuel to the fire of financial pain. This was nothing compared to the physical pain my spouse endured. The emotional devastation inflicted upon me and my family was severe. I avoided bankruptcy and foreclosure, though I'm not confident I comprehend how. Having those sort of things happen is not what someone from my background was accustomed to. I was taught you owe no one and pay for whatever you purchase in life. There could not have been a worse time to build a new home or lose a job.

At forty-one I started over with the children in Texas, as noted. It took almost a year for me to get a Texas medical license. I didn't care to subject myself or the kids to another employer, so I took out an SBA note to start a private practice. I was over forty. Looking back at this, how could I tell my children to expose themselves to something similar unless they felt it was a calling more than a way to make a living? For me the financial and emotional price had been too steep.

For a time, the practice went well. Again I cleared the note and provided a very adequate living space for the children and myself. They had very good high school years. I didn't come from money and hadn't been taught much about it other than you make it, enjoy it, and make some more. Books I have read since I have gotten older certainly give me pause for reflection. These books most often express that timing is everything when it comes to investing, and the most efficient model is a slower gradual gain given time to mature. How sobering when time has passed! For certain, one thing I have learned is that time is all we have, and there is no certainty as to how much. How foolish not to give it its deserved respect. I have told many patients that one thing worse than dying is living and regretting it. Certainly there is no love for self in believing that. People get beaten up in this life and belief that life is no longer worth living is a result of the repetitive trauma. I have recently studied the behavior patterns of those diagnosed with PTSD. I can say I believe I myself qualify to a degree. I have met many who have expressed to me that if they had to go on another day without hope of less pain, they would rather die.

Like most, I remember the nightmare of 2008, which resulted from greed, the politics of deregulation, crooked dealings in the real estate sector, and the decline of the stock market. More than a few lost savings. Some never recovered. For many, losing pensions made the dream of retirement unobtainable, replaced by the nightmare of working until there is no gas left in the tank. Recently a movie was made about it called *The Big Short.*

I bought property to build a clinic. Unfortunately, the property declined in value, and my professional fees at the office dropped 60 percent at the same time. As a single parent, my attentions were diversified, like a good investment should be. Admittedly, my full attention was not on my practice, but on my children at a time when they needed me most. Raising my children, buying cars, and helping them with college were not cheap. However, I wouldn't trade one moment of that for all the money in the world because the lessons on love they taught me were immeasurable, as was my love for them. Others smarter than I lost money, jobs, and homes. Even those considered educated in money management and with millions in stock portfolios felt the pain. It was the worst financial calamity since the Great Depression.

Selling the property at a loss, I fell behind in paying income taxes. I could have used the law to protect the home, but with the kids grown and gone, there seemed to be little reason at the time to keep it. One sure way to stop the excessive IRS penalties was to file for Chapter 7 followed by a Chapter 13 bankruptcy. I believed it was the best thing to do, although it felt like defeat at the time. When the IRS issues penalties, they are not small. I had spent while the harvest was good and attempted to grow my portfolio, but I had not anticipated this near-depression. With all my years of studying, my core curriculum hadn't included business or economic courses geared toward managing a practice. Again, allowing myself to look back, might there have been some way to take on enough work by some other means that would have allowed me to avoid the bankruptcy? Perhaps. I couldn't see it at the time. I remember thinking I had left Missouri confused and angry. I had resolved some of this, believing God would see me through and I would find a way to survive the tragedy. Opening my own practice nurtured this notion for a time. Having it turn upside down reignited the flames of bitterness and anger. I recall thinking, *What must I do to have something turn out good?*

Unlike those with unlimited wealth who have top financial advisors who shield their assets from loss, I did not have help. It still upsets me that even though I had made a good living before the crash, I had nothing material to show for it.

The bankruptcy is over, paid for like the school debt. I remain employed and do have a salary at present comparable to the income of the best years of private practice. That is a blessing. It is almost laughable that a lawsuit came when a few physicians, including me, left a hospital for reasons I will not disclose. It is of public record, but I choose to leave it alone. Let me say we tried to work it out. Medicine has changed, and in order to be profitable, hospitals charge additional fees to try and counter the low insurance payments. Frankly this practice is unethical in my opinion. It worked out in court, and justice did prevail, but the cost of legal fees almost matched the bankruptcy payments. I was not overcharged; this was simply the cost of the legal battle. Despite the legal actions I had chosen not to be involved in years before, the courtroom found me anyway. It was not of my choosing.

Considering this experience and others I've mentioned, I decided to not recommend to the children that they pursue medicine. Others with different experiences would no doubt advise accordingly. If the children felt called into medicine, I would not have stopped them. After all, my youngest is a nurse. I certainly respect her choice and hope she gains satisfaction in helping others. I sincerely believe that because of the changes in medicine, one needs to be called into this as more of a ministry than a money maker, which really should be the cause for healing the sick and afflicted anyway. This is not the place for those expecting overwhelming wealth. Some may still have that, depending on the specialty they choose, but not the majority.

In my final years, I will try to close strong, as I did on the mat and in the ring: save what I can to leave the children something material from my labor. I got nothing materially from my father, but I valued the love he showed me during troubled times as well as good years when he was older.

The best thing I can leave my children is the love and devotion I gave. Those will endure. The money I did and do make would not be a fortune to many. I regret I was not a better caretaker of what I did receive. I feel a sense of shame in that. I did, to my credit, always help anyone in need and gave away a great deal of money as well as spent it. I am glad I was and am willing to give and happy I spent money, especially when it came to the kids and me taking vacations together. I think, like in anything, moderation is the best play. Many have accumulated fortunes only to leave them behind and have the beneficiaries waste them. Others have gathered wealth early and before death given away millions to some great causes. I don't know how their generosity of massive sums could have come early in life unless they began with a fair amount of money to begin with. After all, when people need help, they need it at that moment. If I made mistakes regarding giving, I am satisfied that I did so, rather than being selfish.

I will forever remember the day when I sat before the trustee regarding the bankruptcy. He told me I wasn't the first physician he had met who didn't handle money well, and he desired to hear my explanation. I recalled we had not learned anything about business in school. We had learned biochemistry over and over, never to be used again unless one ventured into research. The best answer I could come up with was something close to this: I tried to be a big fish in a small pond. I ended up squid shit in the ocean. I remember him laughing and indicating he would help me make it as painless as possible.

Since I no longer had a home or clinic to sell, I sold the only thing I had left: me. I am blessed with excellent physical health, and most people find it hard to believe I am sixty. The insurance should replace the home that Tamara and I lost. I wanted to leave them something along with my love. I think this proves that, like it or not, money does matter. I am not complaining about my father. He left me more than enough. The love was all I needed. My children feel the same. Yet I know the financial trouble I have had, some of it my own fault. I desire better for them. In death as in life, I will do what I can to help them financially, while understanding that giving too much financially can lessen a person's energy to make their own money.

A man once said to me, "I hope you make only as much money as you can handle well." I apparently exceeded that amount. For those of you who are fellow members of this club, I salute you! I would offer pity and regret, but it won't help. Again, let us believe this made us better souls. Many of the Christian faith and others are taught the love of money is a great sin. It is needed to survive, but the worship of it over a higher power appears to have ruined the characters of many. The love of things is not thought of as a great value by God. As great as love is, when it is misplaced, even love can create pain. Then again, that is not holy and just love, is it?

There was another investment called LIFT. I can assure you it didn't end up like the old hymn "Love Lifted Me!" It an acronym for life insurance funding transactions. The idea was a decent one. Life insurance policies were written on employees and signed over to the employer. The money was to fund pensions that have now disappeared. AIG bank was in the process of underwriting the effort, and there was much interest from several companies. AIG declared bankruptcy about that time. The government saw fit to offer bailouts, with CEOs getting paid huge options. I came close to a windfall, but no cigar, nor an ashtray to place it in.

I made this effort to be made whole. If insurance had taken me out of practice, then the idea that this investment could make it possible for me to practice medicine less so that I might invest time elsewhere was a pleasant idea. Failing wasn't from a lack of effort. If anything, the efforts I made actually resulted in a poor outcome. They say life is a risky business. I would have to agree. Sometimes a risk pays a dividend, but it's not nice at all when the opposite occurs. It is ironic, but the day I declared bankruptcy was the same time I discovered what true wealth meant. Wealth should not be measured in dollars but, rather, in the love one has given.

The constant reminder of failing is not holy. There are times to play the hand that has been dealt and times to fold. There are also times to decide not to play at all. Many have held steady in life despite what fate dealt and ended up better off for it. For those who held steady while holding on to love, I salute you. For the rest, like me, it is not too late! Love still waits. Forever! What is the message? Over and over: you are not alone. Love is waiting! True and unconditional love is not expensive to purchase. The fact is, if it is real, it is free.

I had a man tell me once, "I can endure about anything but not financial ruin." He died of a heart attack shortly after a financial setback. Why did I include this chapter? Once again to let you as the reader understand you are not alone. No matter what you have withstood, there is someone else out there experiencing the same.

Here is the point: If you and another person met after each experiencing tragedy, and you held each other in your arms, would the two of you feel better or worse? I say better! That is why if you continue to love, you have not failed. Rather you took on failure and turned it into an opportunity to love. Since love is the only thing that will endure, you are in fact successful. Love is the oasis of rest from life's realities.

CHAPTER 15

HOLLYWOOD
Love finds no value in vanity

Love is the greatest refreshment in life.

—Pablo Picasso

I never really had the time to grieve as I would have liked over my mate's death. Some was done along the journey of losing Tamara. There was so much to do, however, because for a time, until the hospital decided otherwise, I was working. The hospital never fired me. Asking me to take a leave of absence without pay was for me a financial disaster considering what the children, Tamara, and I were enduring. I was confused and lost. There were medical expenses, the children, and their needs during this most difficult time. Tamara continued to parent right up to her last breath. The church offered a tremendous amount of help, and Tamara's folks came often and spent as much time as they could. God bless their souls for that. To this day I mourn with them over the loss of their daughter. They are strong people. My dad and stepmom came a few times. Dad drove over and held Tamara's hand all night long shortly before she died. I am so thankful I was able to know he loved her, and he showed it with this action. Toward Tamara's end, there was hospice. It was very stressful and exhausting. Simply put, it hurt!

After the relocation to Texas and during the time of my private practice, there came a time when things had settled down. I began to lie awake at night, however, my thoughts racing. It was upsetting. I finally had time for the pain of the experience to settle in.

One night I got on the computer and started writing. I now understand it was a method of grieving. I started with a novel and at some point bought a software program and began to convert the novel into a screenplay. Over the years, as I became less enchanted with medicine, I found myself watching movie after movie; my creative side began to take over. I wanted to write more. I had an interest in acting, but that seemed out of reach, given my responsibilities. Writing, however, could be done at any time, even in the middle of a sleepless night.

I also found myself from time to time playing the piano again. I recalled the college literature professor who had told me I had the name of another noted writer and the talent to do the same. And the chemistry professor who had called me in to tell me I needed to change my college curriculum. He'd said I wasn't smart enough to be a physician. Between proving him wrong and my mother's wishes, I became a doctor. The time had come to explore my talent as a writer.

I wrote my way through the grieving process. The writing took on a life of its own. I expressed hatred. The pages revealed anger, then resolution. The story started rough. I wrote about a physician who had lost his wife to cancer and in his grief turned to alcohol. In the process he witnessed a murder and was forced to go to the police, and in doing so he embarked on a journey that helped him find peace with God regarding his loss.

The story was 50 to 60 percent true and the rest a web of fiction. I found it interesting and very therapeutic. The process was painful, yet this was the expression I needed. I'd had no time for writing until then. It was the beginning of peace, yet the result was again frustration in many ways. During this time my middle child, my daughter Ali, was expressing herself in school plays and musicals. Her voice became so beautiful that I asked her to consider finding some musicians and making a CD. Ali is extremely talented. She wrote lyrics and melodies, and soon she had us meeting with very talented musicians. She booked a studio, and her CD of five songs was completed.

The songs and the expression of her talent were nothing less than extraordinary. She developed a web page and expressed the desire to act. I still believe her songs are good enough to take to a record label, but she became more interested in acting and got work in several movies. Perhaps one day she will be able to express love through her beautiful voice while acting as well. Recently she has done some public speaking and developed online teaching courses. Nothing she chooses defines her. It is her journey, and if there is one thing I have learned, it is to encourage but not to choose someone else's journey for them. There is but one life here. It is sacred. There are no do-overs, and turning right versus left can change the experience from a joyful ride to a flat tire!

Before and during this time, Ali worked at the local mall. How I miss those days. Her younger sister, Gentry, and I would sometimes wait for her to get off work so we could all go get coffee and tea together. A few times we went into the clothing store, and while Gentry was shopping around, I would be in some distant corner watching Ali work. What a treat that was. One night a tall, handsome young man came in. Soon I saw he was talking to my daughter. I didn't care for it much and wondered what the deal was. After the store closed, I asked Ali about him. She said he was looking for a model for a shoot he was doing and wanted her to go to his house. That went over like a lead balloon, and immediately I let her know she certainly would not be going without me!

The day came, and we went. I thought for sure I would be meeting someone who had bad intentions for my daughter, and he was about to get the surprise of his life. Instead I got the surprise of mine. Jason and his wife,

Kelsey, are wonderful people and are now two of my best friends. They just attended, after all these years, Ali and Bobby's wedding. It was wonderful to see them again.

Ali completed the modeling shoot with Jason, and he has gone on to develop quite a marketing business. He is so multitalented I could not even begin to explain. I asked him, since he was working in video, if he would like to shoot a music video for my daughter. I really thought the song she had dedicated to her mother would be a wonderful video and might help her in some way while being a great gift to me. The video is simply beautiful, a tribute to Tamara. Our family is all in the video, and I believe it helped us express our love for her in an everlasting way.

After the video was completed, I dug out my dusty screenplay and, in another moment of insanity, asked Jason if he thought we could shoot a full feature film. My goodness! We certainly had no idea what we were biting off. We bought cameras, whether I could afford them or not. We also obtained a lighting kit, microphones, booms, and a trailer we customized to haul everything. Looking back, it was unreal. Next we were in contact with a talent agent in Dallas. Ali and Jason were already acquainted with her. I cannot believe we held casting calls for the characters in our house. Our moviemaking experience had begun.

For two years we ran around Fort Worth and Arlington, Texas, on the weekends, securing bars, houses, coffee shops, and even a local police station where we shot scenes. I played myself, and local acting talent along with a cast of family and friends helped us complete the project. After we shot all the footage (over sixty hours), we got bogged down in editing. We'd had no idea how incredibly difficult sound would prove to be. We had shot some scenes in places that were open for business, and now we understood what "quiet on the set" meant, as every sound was picked up by the microphones. However, this film was meant to be, because just as our crew of three was about to surrender, I went in to change an insurance policy. The Allstate agent was curious when I asked him about insurance for a trailer to haul our equipment in. As it turned out, John had worked as an instructor for a software editing program called Pro Tools, so our crew quickly became four. We went so far as to build a sound box and place it in John and his wife Lois's living room for a year, and actors were brought back to repeat their lines and complete voice-overs. With the crew of four and the help of anyone we could find, we finished the film, which we titled *Between Heaven and Hell.*

Our budget was less than $100,000. I secured music from A-list stars. There is some beautiful music in the film. Bruce Springsteen's label was very easy to work with. To have other songs by Kris Kristofferson and Leonard Cohen was a blessing. We were fortunate to have some good acting too. There were actors such as James Grant, Dennis O'Neill, and Andrew Sensenig, who had been in many films. It's interesting now that my daughter has gone on to be in much bigger and better productions. But for me it was never about anything but the message. It was the message in the story that I believed could help others change or at the least modify their choices in life. The film was released for DVD at the time.

We did play it twice in Dallas-Fort Worth theaters, and people had to be turned away each time. It received attention and had got good reviews. We entered it in a festival and obtained distribution. Our production team were interviewed by various media entities. When watching these interviews again, I am amazed by how well we expressed ourselves about our efforts. Blockbuster ordered thousands of copies of the movie, and for a minute—like the time found myself in Barnes and Noble signing the book of shorts I had written and now rewritten—I thought this would sell on the DVD shelf, and money would be made. This time we could get more help and make a second film better considering all we had learned.

Suddenly the lines at Blockbuster were gone. The orders were canceled. Netflix and video on demand were the new thing. We ran out of time, energy, and money. It has been on the Internet Movie Database and received good reviews, and even now patients and others ask about it and want copies. As I said before, timing is everything, and I seemed to have little knack for it. Now, after a decade and with some additional effort, the movie is on Amazon Prime, Xbox, iTunes, and a few other internet platforms. I have seen much worse, movies with no message at all. For what we lacked in money and experience, what we pulled off was astounding. In an attempt to make it real, we used some language that is offensive to some. But that is all it is: a form of expression. I thought it helped to make the moral issues that were resolved more powerful in the end.

I had my moment with Hollywood. I believe my daughter will have a much greater one should she desire it. None of us know when God will ring our final bell. I do know I got to sit next to Bobby, Ali's spouse, when we were in Nashville for the red-carpet event for Ali's lead role in the movie *The Song*. It played in theaters and was here for a month in Kansas City. The words Ali expressed at the end of her red-carpet affair were all I will ever need to hear. They were no more than a simple "Thank you" for being there. Taylor and Gentry were in LA for the red carpet with her for her part in *Twilight*. No matter what Ali decides to do, I know she will do well, for, like me, she gives it her best.

Would I do it again? Yes, I would. I did apologize to Jason and John for putting them and their families through it. They declined to accept the apology, as they too felt it had been worth it. From the movie to the ring, the journey had been worth it—all part of the *gift* we have been given. The gift of life. Its joy. Its pain. The call of God. The will of a higher being. Our part in something so vast: the universe! At this point it would seem fate may not permit me the opportunity to give an acceptance speech for some award regarding my efforts in life. If it ever does, I think it would go something like this:

Thanks to my mother, who, in taking her life, taught me to attempt to live mine. To my dad, who showed me there was no shame in being common. To my in-laws, who showed me kindness. To my children, who forced me to be unselfish despite myself and who returned love despite my weaknesses. To my wife, who gave me those individuals and whose love as a woman was healing and provided warmth. To friends who cared. To my patients, who allowed me to treat and learn from them. Finally, to my Father in heaven, who provides a place to dwell outside earth where time will not abide. A place where love is abundant and unconditional.

The ironic thing in doing this movie was that it allowed me to grieve. Then it became a project. The movie did not return the money spent and allow for the making of another. I understood it could end up being yet another excuse to become bitter or angry. Another curse of wrong timing and reasoning to believe there wasn't anything I could do correctly at the right time. I fought hard not to let that happen. As much as I was able to, this time I accepted fate. Even though I would try to do my best to get the movie seen, I would not allow it to become another negative. After all, it was to be a work of art and an expression of greater understanding. It was about acceptance and unconditional love. The fact it was ever completed was a miracle in itself.

If failure is not to try, we at least were not guilty of that. We did not let fear erase our efforts to be productive. Sure, I had some regrets, mostly for others who gave so much of their time and love. Having learned so much, it was hard to accept knowledge wasted. Despite that, I found a sense of pride in making it. From what I have been told, it was a blessing to the majority who saw it. Those who caught the message. It caused them to think about the choices they make while here in this life, and that was the intent.

Recently, and ironically, I saw a movie titled *Choices*. Some things were similar to our movie. In some ways it was better than what I wrote, in large part because it was done with *love*. I may have allowed too much bitterness and anger to reveal itself before I let love in. In my attempt to make it real, there may have been too much ugly for some to endure before love was allowed to make the difference. If I didn't know better, I would have thought someone saw mine and asked, how can we improve upon this work? They undoubtedly had a higher budget and had experience as well. They allowed pain in, but love always remained. From beginning to end, the evidence of love was apparent.

My story revealed the loss of love for a time. This does happen, but it can be hard to watch. That should teach us what reality should be. No matter how difficult the loss, it is far better not to lose sight of love!

I am confident your story has some painful and ugly memories. If not, either you have learned the secret of letting go or, up to this time, have been extremely blessed. If your story is in some ways like mine, you, as I did, will have to face it or be run over by it. I suggest you face it head-on and let love help you look at the memories and smile, for you are you, and the memory has made you, made you find the reason to love. Love gives you the chance to make the last chapter a good one, to close the book with admiration that you fought through the pain and in doing so showed others the light of love in your eyes. Dare to love. Dare to leave the memory of it behind for those you love after you have gone home. Our lives here begin and end. What lies in between is the journey. The experience requires choices. Let the choices be motivated by *love*! I have recently met a woman. I never have seen her frown or reveal sorrow. She is one of those people who appears to have had a perfect life and her smile is forever beaming. After talking to her, I realized her life had been quite the opposite. I asked her how she managed to pull this off. Her answer was a reflection of the movie I produced. She had made a choice to never let anyone see the pain but only joy—an example of tough resolve. Her message is her gift to the world! I will be forever humbled by the never-ending smile of Kathleen. She chose love!

Here is the plain and simple truth. I have every reason or excuse, depending on how one examines the issue, to be extremely bitter, very angry, and full of jealousy for those who seem to have lived a blessed life, though I'm certain they have had difficulties. I am very aware of and thankful for my physical health, for which I express gratitude toward God. Yet the sustained emotional, mental, and psychological beatings have given me pause to believe at times I am alive only to be tortured. Honestly, after praying and meditating over God's word claiming and humbly asking for restoration, only to have more beatings come, I don't believe anymore in many of those promises. That's the honest truth. This is one of the reasons this writing is different, not full of pretense. Even so, I refuse not to continue loving. This is why: The emotions mentioned above do nothing to help anyone, not me or another. They are only ugly at best. Here is the main reason: Christ did nothing to anger anyone. He was not unfair or unjust. The Bible indicates he only helped and in some cases healed the afflicted. Pilate washed his hands with the matter of his crucifixion. He was innocent yet crucified. And since his last plea was to ask his father to forgive those who knew not what they were doing in death, he loved. Why?

He indicated it was the greatest of his commands. Despite my sacrifices and my tortured disappointments in my life, I love. I love because I can testify that it makes all the difference in the world. I have never hugged, kissed, or told anyone that I loved them that it didn't change their day for the better. I saw it in their eyes, their movement, their amazement. Even at times the lack of a word spoken revealed it.

I do it because I choose to. I pray it is the last thing I do before I die. I am not promising you anything. I'm making no guarantee of abundance, of money, wealth, or fame. I have none myself. It has been taken at every turn. Even those I loved were gone early and before I expected. While I remained bitter and angry, I saw the destruction it brought. When I forced myself to love, it changed. After a while I didn't have to force it anymore. Love changes lives. Some people have never felt love. As such they grew up hard and didn't care what they did or whom they did it to. The harshness or lack of love was most likely part of the reason they went insane! I have never seen a case when, if all else fails, love does not at least offer a chance.

More than once I wished I would never wake up. I was far too tired and beaten to desire within myself to live another day. But I got up. Why? For yet another chance to love someone who was less fortunate than myself.

Some will say, "This has nothing to do with me. I don't believe in Christ. I serve a different God. My religion is different." That is not the point. The point is *love*. Without love I don't care whom or what you serve. You have nothing! Nothing at all! You are only serving yourself!

CHAPTER 16

SOBRIETY

Cultivating love requires clear judgment

There is no remedy for love but to love more.

—*Henry David Thoreau*

I promised myself I would never have alcohol in my home. I didn't have good memories associated with it. I chose not to have it around my children or my woman. She and I made that stick. Tamara and I shared a beach drink or two along the way, but we stayed away from the bar-and-club scene. Both of us had had brief runs with that before we met. We concluded it got us nowhere. The children didn't grow up with much fighting, yelling, or screaming, certainly not compared to what I had experienced. Nothing physical other than the discipline they received, which to this day I think did them no harm because it was very controlled. Tamara and I did our best. If any of my children have children, then their chances will come to do better, and I hope they do. At times it seems that if there is something I did teach the children, it was to wait until later in life to have children—or in fact, based on what they saw me go through, to never have them at all.

I started drinking somewhere around the time of making the movie. I did it for a few of the scenes initially. During that time, I also began to experience some irregularity of my gastro-intestinal system. It was like an old surgeon I'd worked with in my training once said: some "mischief" of the bowel. I had a colonoscopy done; it was negative, and the problem was written off to stress. No doubt I had experienced plenty of that! My recollection would put this drinking phase after the age of fifty. It did help with my intestinal issues initially. At first it was controlled, but over time, quite frankly, it became an issue. What started as something utilized to relieve stress added more of it. Despite being confined to weekends for the most part, it became a problem I would simply need to resolve.

When we were filming the beginning of the movie, we rented out a bar and had it closed so we could bring in all our actors and extras for the scene. I was supposed to be drunk in this scene, but, as it turned out, I got drunker than I was supposed to be. Someone left the door unlocked, and a motorbike gang walked in. They had traveled some distance and wanted beer. They didn't care that we were making a movie. We were outnumbered, and I felt we could be at risk, so there was nothing to do but talk to the leader of the pack. I told him that as hard as it might be to believe, we were making a film, and the bar was, truthfully, closed. He told me they weren't leaving without beer, so we made a deal. I would serve the beer if they would each have one and go. If they agreed, there was no need to call to the police.

My daughters were there as well as some dear friends. Some of the male extras hadn't arrived yet. Thank God the leader agreed, but after they finished their beers, it wasn't quite over. The leader came over to me and thanked me for the beer but said he wouldn't leave until I shared a drink with him. With that he pulled a flask from his vest. I told him he would have to drink it first. I had no intention of being poisoned to death. He took a drink and handed it to me. I did the same. When I handed it back, he said, "You're all right. Good luck with the movie." They were gone, and the door was then locked for sure.

The night continued, and we shot and reshot scenes, as Jason's idea of perfection was to shoot until death. He did do a great job, however. Somewhere in this process, I got lost. To this day I don't know if I had one too many trying to make the scene a little too real or if there was more than I bargained for in the biker's flask. I do know that before the night was over, I was being propped up at the bar. I could barely speak the lines and had to be awakened to do so. As I was told later, I said a few things that were not in very good taste to the costars. They had mercy on me, thankfully.

Finally, the night of shooting film was over. My daughters and Jason dragged me to the car. They took me home and placed me in the shower, where I vomited, cried, and completely humiliated myself. I'm so glad they loved me. People refer to the romance of booze. This was not one of those nights. From that point on, I would have a drink now and then, sometimes a little more than other times. Was it pent up anxiety, stress, and disappointment? At that point I was in a semi-controlled decline.

Over the next few years and after the children were out on their own, my drinking was limited to a couple of scotches infrequently. Eventually, I found excuses to find the liquor store on weekends. Liquor settled my nerves, or so I thought, and as long as I was home, I assumed no one no one could be hurt but me. I was alone except for the dogs.

Unfortunately, I failed to hide or shut off the cell phone. Like others who had fallen into this trap, I began drunk calling a few friends and the children. My depression over the losses in life combined with trials and troubles were without a doubt enhanced by the addition of a very good depressant. The liquor did its job well, so naturally I got more depressed. I talked of misery, pain, and even my death—just what anyone and everyone wanted and needed to hear. It was purely selfish. I had reasoned with sanity and sobriety that there were people this planet would be better off without. Now, as a drunk without any reasoning at all, I concluded I was one of them. It became obvious this self-pity was nothing more than a poor choice and an excuse for cowardice.

Those who cared and loved me confronted me. They let me know they understood why I felt so despondent, but my actions were not helping me. It took a little time to see they were correct. I attended a Tony Robbins conference, and he did nothing but help me see what I was allowing to happen. I listened to what my friends said and suffered terrible remorse when my older daughter called and told me I had phoned her and said some terrible things. I didn't remember any of it. Ali was firm and strong. She didn't mince words. Her love for me was there. She simply told me to stop unless I wanted to lose what we had.

Gentry didn't care for it either. My son indicated he wasn't going to judge me. He felt he couldn't he after what he had done. Still, he knew where I was headed, because he had been there. Other drugs besides alcohol were involved, but this one is far easier. Why? Because it is legal. Some can drink responsibly, while others drink and drive and kill innocent people. Most people think it's OK to drink as long as they have rides home, but no one really talks about what happens when alcohol causes you to sink into the depths of depression. Getting home doesn't mean the horrible effects on family and relationships end.

I apologized to the children for this time of weakness in my life and offered apologies to anyone else I may have offended. I never risked my medical license or impaired my judgment in caring for patients. I was a weekend warrior. It hurt me that I had fallen prey to this seduction that can turn into a form of evil. But it was easy for me to put it down. I did it quickly, and it will never touch my lips again. No classes needed. The embarrassment was enough for me. I will never drink again. While attending a meeting alongside my son, I read over the twelve steps. I gathered that I had done them unknowingly. I was no better than anyone else there. If drugs or alcohol cause pain, there is a problem.

How many have been hurt by alcohol? Many. What I noticed after I stopped drinking and started observing others is just how much alcohol some people drink. I now sit at restaurant tables watching the bar area from a distance. I never took notice of it before, but some people drink a lot of alcohol. So many have been killed by drunk drivers (who usually seem to survive). How many deaths have there been from marijuana? Far fewer than alcohol! Legitimate medical uses have been discovered. People drive twenty-five miles per hour instead of a hundred if impaired. Some studies indicate a glass of wine is good for your health, but that doesn't mean an entire bottle is better. Opiates that I prescribe for pain help many people, but there is always the potential for abuse when patients don't follow directions and orders. That makes it hard on the clinician and patients who need help. Some see marijuana a gateway drug. I see little difference in that belief when compared to alcohol. People make a choice to abuse or not! Politicians debate it. I do know alcohol has a proven track record, and that it certainly is not good.

I recently attended an academy for citizens held by the local sheriff's department. It was designed to help citizens understand the difficulties of police work. I wanted to understand because of my son's troubles and my own interest in the law. Our last class discussed DUIs, and I can't describe the graphic pictures I saw of victims of those driving under the influence of alcohol. It made me ill, and all I could do when I left was call my son and tell him how thankful I am that he is alive. I am appreciative to the officers and personnel who gave their time for the program. I learned a lot. God bless the officers and their families. They didn't have a reserve program. If they did, I would have joined.

I took my son to Las Vegas for his twenty-first birthday so I could dance and drink with him. Was it fun? Sure. Was it the best choice? Looking back, it wasn't. All of us recently went to Idaho. We rented a cabin, rafted the white water, and rode horses in the mountains. I can without reservation tell you it was more fun than Las Vegas. Not that seeing great entertainers is not wonderful, but appreciating the wonder and beauty of God rather than pouring poison down one's throat is much kinder and wiser for certain. Some of the best times can not only be ruined by drugs and alcohol but missed altogether.

Everything in moderation, the Bible indicates. There is nothing wrong with a father and son sharing a beer together or a mother and daughter enjoying a glass of wine. The problem is that moderation goes out the window for some. If you have ever been embarrassed by your actions or been in trouble with the law because of drinking, you need to stop drinking. You have crossed the line, and you are headed for a life of misery—if you are fortunate enough to live. Life is a gift. Life with love is the greatest gift. I believe love is best and fully experienced sober. No one is perfect, as I'm sure most would agree. Some might say or add, "I am perfect through Christ or God" (or some higher power they choose). I remain convinced most would agree that in and of ourselves, we are not perfect.

Life can and does throw many curves at us. There are joys and sorrows, great highs and lows. Anxiety and stress are known to many. People seek help or sometimes try to deal with it on their own. I repeat: we don't all share the same backgrounds or experiences.

For me, and what appears to be more than a few others, drugs and alcohol can be a slippery slope. From one human to another, moving ahead with caution is sound advice.

Life and love are so precious. With love as a guide, I think we do life justice by offering ourselves and others our best. Each of us bears the responsibility of measuring that. It was love that stopped me from drinking: Love for my children. Love for the memory of their mother. Love for a higher power. Respect and love for those who have given their lives so we could live in freedom. Love for myself. Love and respect for others who have suffered through grief and loss due to alcohol. It was love that tamed the beast—the beast in me.

If you read this and decide a beast remains in you, try love. It will call to you. If you hear and accept the call, you can and will tame the beast. Any beast can be confined to the cage in which it belongs. It can be forever caged, not a beast any longer. From a lion to a lamb. This and more with the help of love. You are not alone! We all struggle. We fight to remain sane in an insane world. We suffer, endure hardship and loss. Then we experience joy, kindness, and mercy. This is life as we know it here in this world. Do your best to let your light shine. Where there is light, there is love!

There are many addictions and hardships that life lays in front of us. Not everyone makes it out alive. It is remarkable how many talented and famous people, as well as those who are neither, have fallen prey to this disease of addiction. My son witnessed a young man die in front of his eyes after overdosing in a sober living house. I as well as others have paid enormous sums of money for rehab/detox and sober living facilities. Honestly the success rate of several can be questioned. I myself have wondered if any of them served any purpose at all other than taking money for a job poorly done. Despite that, there are a few that do all they can. The fact is that in the end, the choice is up to the individual. Does he have enough love for family? Enough respect for himself? Faith enough that a higher power cares? I once again maintain that support is needed, and love is the best chance for a complete change. One day the afflicted person simply decides to love living. They surrender the addiction and choose differently. At first it may be one day at a time. But eventually the mere idea of what he was sickens him. At that point he knows he now loves himself enough to have a fighting chance for recovery. A boxer can have the best trainer, the best mentor, the best cut-man. When the bell rings, though, the fight is his alone. It is the will to never surrender and to get up off the canvas that separates the very good from the great, the champions who refuse to surrender. It is the love of winning at all costs, the love of no surrender, that wins in the end.

During times of depression and loss, especially when we are alone, our minds become fertile ground for the seeds of bitterness, anger, and despair to take root. Such seeds can take time to grow, but they eventually will if they are watered by self-pity. The wounds these emotions create for yourself and others that love you are powerful. This demise must be stopped. The ground must be re-plowed and the seeds of love sown to replace those of negativity.

There isn't anything *love can't change*!

CHAPTER 17

MOMENT OF FOREVER

Forever is the majesty of love

Love doesn't make the world go round.
Love is what makes the ride worthwhile.

—*Franklin P. Jones*

The time came for my middle child's wedding. She was the first of my three children to embark upon this journey. I had been confident the day would come, but honestly, there was no way for me to be ready. This was time of hopeful expectation, with my desire for her dreams to come true and intense faith that the events of life would be kind and merciful to her and her chosen soul mate.

I guarded my words carefully. I tried to make sure my presence was considered positive and that I was not packing any negativity in my suitcase. I attempted to hide any pain in not having her mother there. Regardless I understood my daughter's realization of the same. I made the journey with the idea of being strong and there for her while representing her mother as well. I was concerned that due to health issues, her mother's parents might not make it. Her mother's sister and Uncle Don were coming. Best of all, I had Ali's siblings. My son and other daughter would be there, and, of course, a slew of friends and the new family we were joining. Here it was: the time to hand my precious daughter over to another's care and love. My little girl. My princess.

There was a flood of memories and emotions from the time I arrived and laid eyes on her: The little angel I had pushed on the swing set. Our walks to the local store to gather up her favorite lemon drops—or was it Skittles? Remembering how her brother and she had fought over which was better all the way to the store. Her face landing in the spaghetti while sleeping at the dinner table. Her famous screams that left little doubt for her mother and me that those pipes would allow her to sing.

I remembered her first horse ride, which left her laughing hysterically when the gray bucked and reared. Ali expressed no fear, while I ran for the reins. The time she backed into a mailbox with the truck she loved, and her hesitant phone call to let me know. Our times in the house when she and her siblings carried on my family tradition of scaring one another half to death at any opportunity with "Boo" or "Got ya!" The pool parties. The all-night sleep overs with her girlfriends. These and so much more, all in the past now. The time to move on into another chapter. Could I measure up one more time? Make sure she had the joy she deserved without the weeping, mortified dad? They were tears of joy, not agonizing sorrow: the acceptance of gaining a son and a new family and not losing a daughter.

Soon I was in the airport and walking to the gate. There were Kathy and Uncle Don. The grandfolks were there! Thank God they'd made it. Grandma was in a wheelchair but had a big smile on her face. She wasn't going to miss the wedding. We made our flight, and the trip was smooth. We all got our rides, and soon we were unpacking at the hotel and getting the schedule down. In a blur we were at the rehearsal and dinner that followed. So many people were there: The girls who once had slumbered on beds and floors. The family who had come with me, along with the soon-to-be new ones.

My heart was beating fast, but I had not counted on what I noticed first. Ali was in her mother's wedding dress, which had been her grandmother's as well, for the rehearsal. I was proud that Ali was embracing the memory of her mother and filled with joy in knowing Tamara was there. Ali displayed the courage to make sure of that. She looked so much like her mother. Then my dear Gentry. She was in the dress her mother had worn on our ten-year delayed honeymoon. They both had their mother's features in unique and different ways.

I was so incredibly moved by their strength and desire to honor not only Tamara but me as well. Not a selfish bone to be found. I was spellbound yet knew in a moment that my confirmation had come. It was righteous, and I had done a good job. At that moment, doubts about my performance as a parent were erased for a time. Who was there at my side to offer more encouragement and strength but my son, Taylor—the one with the troubled spirit, now with quiet reverence and offering support to the father who had been there for him. He was now returning the favor with strength and courage. What an honor! The grandfolks, uncle, and aunt—all there with bushels of love. The new family so kind and loving. My soon-to-be new son, with his brother there. Bobby so happy and full. Ali was in good hands, and his love for and devotion to her were without question.

The rehearsal was full of just plain fun and incredible joy. I was fine. It was all going to be just fine. I didn't expect speeches; I guess I thought that might be post wedding, at the reception, but it worked out very well. With the dancing, visitation, and cutting of the cake at the reception, it did make sense to offer words at a calmer moment. Bobby has a huge family and even more friends. I think he had about fourteen groomsmen, many young men who thought a great deal of him. It was obvious even at that relatively young age that both he and Ali had already touched many lives. Many made speeches at the rehearsal dinner, and their words were majestic. Bobby's folks preceded me, and there was great love and humor. Bobby's father, Nari, was amusing as he spoke of his son with a great deal of humor and love. Bobby took it all very well.

My time came. I had no speech prepared. I stood and offered some comic relief, with Bobby's father by my side. I then moved on to words that came from my heart and soul. To this day I cannot recall all I said. I remember tears from many in the room. Some told me afterward it had been so inspirational and moving, it would be remembered as a spiritual event. I really can't say what I uttered. I believe it came from God, Tamara, and the part of me that was unseen. I do remember kissing Bobby and Ali and letting Ali know I would give my life for her without hesitation. Other than that, the words will remain there and in the hearts of those in attendance. At least it seemed Ali and Bobby were satisfied. Apparently I didn't embarrass them or myself. Mission accomplished!

My son stood. He didn't say too much, but what he did say was a powerful admission of struggles but purpose for a future. The champion fighter he was and is came through again. That brought me to tears. The joy for my daughter and her lover, the strength of her sister and their brother—it was more than I could have asked for.

There were words from Bobby's older brother, Tony, recalling his memories of former days and the admiration he had for both his brother and his new sister. Grandpa fought back tears and called us over for a more private moment. It seemed that while he was visiting his daughter's (Tamara's) grave, he had found four carpenter nails. He searched hard and couldn't find any others. He had them cleaned and placed each on a rope necklace. Always a humble man, he presented them to us—another confirmation that, as I said to Ali, Tamara was there.

The wedding was, in the words of Tony Robbins, a life-changing, massive action of love. Unconditional love. Bobby and Ali were radiant. The bridesmaids were not slumbering now, especially with the visiting bee that became interested in their flowers. Gentry took care of the bee. The fourteen groomsmen seemed like a small army of pride and love. The look on my son's face when I smiled and said, *"You drive her up, son"* brought a radiant smile from him, one that had disappeared for a while during his years of trouble. There it was, better than ever!

I never saw Gentry give the ring to Tony. It seemed in the moment, Bobby's brother had forgotten it. Gentry had shown it to me beforehand and smiled. At some point while beautiful words of promise and enduring, faithful love were being expressed by my daughter and new son, she had managed to move with ghostlike precision and put the ring in the right hands.

So there, among the love, joy, and tears, were the new couple. It was done. My daughter had promised her love to a dear young man and he to her. The contract. The commitment. It was theirs. A moment of forever.

The reception, the food, the cake! Friends and family. Dancing with the girls I had once seen cuddled together in slumber-party bliss. They are grown women now, some with children of their own. I was so glad that Ali had let me choose a few songs for the DJ, so I could show that the older man could still shake a leg. So many dear friends. It was good to see them and how they expressed their love.

Gentry had saved her words for the reception, and she delivered them at the appropriate time. In accordance with her style, they were solid and pure, full of strength and humor. There was no hesitation in the love she expressed for Ali and Bobby.

My dance came, the one with my dear daughter. She had asked me a month earlier what I would like to dance to. I suggested "A Moment of Forever" by Kris Kristofferson.

Ali had said, "Dad, I chose that song for us two years ago."

So we danced. I held on to the daughter I *loved* so much and the picture of my own soul mate, who had joined the universe and God twenty years earlier. I sang along with Kris. I made the most of my moment of forever. It was a moment I hold on to today in my mind whenever I close my eyes.

My sixtieth birthday was a week after my return home. I had asked for it to go unnoticed. This was Ali and Bobby's time, not mine. But again the unselfish love shone through. Taylor asked me to go look at the apartment gym with him, and there they were: a handful of friends and Bobby, Ali, Tony, and Gentry. Family. All gathered with gifts and a cake, to take time out to celebrate with me. How could a father ever doubt the love of his children? I have at times, but those times are long gone.

On the plane going home, or what I call home for now, I played the song Ali and I had danced to on my iPod a few times. I closed my eyes and thought of the time. The journey. The beginning. Days gone by. A love that survived through the pain, through the losses and the gains. The memories. Only one thing remained. One thing brought healing. One thing was eternal. It is true: love quiets the beast. Love is the greatest gift. Love grants us mercy. Forgiveness. Understanding. Eternal hope. Faith.

I was told the dance was fitting. Powerful. Enduring. Emotional. It was what it was. It is what it is. A moment of forever! Thank you, Ali and Bobby. Thank you very much for sharing. I love you.

Many of you have given up your angels to others in marriage. During and after the event, what did you hope for more than anything? That they truly and deeply loved each other. Why? Because you knew that was all that really mattered. I know you understand.

Now my younger daughter has married as well. Her and Zachery's wedding was quite different from Bobby and Ali's. It was smaller, located on the Finger Lakes about an hour outside Syracuse, New York, with crystal-clear water and simply some of the most beautiful country in the United States. They had a small, intimate ceremony beside Lake Otisco at the family camp. The ceremony was beautiful, like Ali's, just in a different way. After words and vows were exchanged, Gentry and Zach ran down the pier and jumped into the water. They indeed were literally jumping into marriage. Ali, Gentry, and I danced later under the tent prepared for the gathering. The band was really good, and man, did the three of us get down. We laughed and danced, and, to say the least, my girls are hilarious! Gentry and I almost passed out watching Ali!

Once again, love. Great love. Love was dancing all around us, and so were we. Zachary. His brothers. His folks. Bob and Lynn. Just wonderful. I went parasailing with Bob. My God, that was one of the best days of my life.

There is nothing like love ! Truth and love. It is all we need. It is truly all we ever needed.

For those of you who have experienced both the joy and sorrow of moments like these, understand you are not alone. When parents give everything, when they sacrifice their dreams and desires as individuals, because they dared to love a woman or man and have children, I admire them—especially when a mate dies and one parent is left to do the job alone, or the parents are divorced and one is abandoned to push forth by him- or herself. The time comes when the reality of giving your child away hits home. No longer do the phone calls come as before. There are few texts, and maybe not even a request for advice. Another has taken that place. The children's lives are their own now, and the reality that you only had them on loan settles in. This is an entirely new adjustment to deal with. With no mate to turn to, no life of your own, the sense of emptiness comes.

In time love may circle back. There is little doubt love is displaced for a while. Credit for many things given to a spouse that wasn't there to do what we did for years prior. I advise you to consider yourself, to love yourself enough to find reasons to love life even when alone. For without love life can become harsh and cold. Warm yourself when you can with love, like a blanket on a cold night. It is simply not worth living without it! For those who haven't found someone yet to share love with, you can volunteer your services. Go give love. Give to family. A child. A nephew, a niece. Don't despair. In doing these things, love will find you. Your miracle can come with another who is looking. You are not alone. Someone is looking just like you are!

CHAPTER 18

SOUL MATES

Souls unite when love is true

Love is composed of a single soul
inhabiting two bodies.

—*Aristotle*

U p to this point, I haven't mentioned much about
how Tamara and I met. I'm getting around to it. It
took time before the children and I talked about what
they remember regarding their mother. As the adult I
knew the last few years were full of pain, and I imagined from a child's point of view it was like a horror
film. I shouldn't wonder why later my daughter would
have trouble acting in horror films. Of course, children
are much tougher than we give them credit for. Their
mother remained very strong and died with courage

and dignity well beyond the circumstances. I have considered myself possibly wrong about my children's feelings surrounding Tamara's death.

Recently, for example, my middle child shared with me a few things she remembered about her mother. Her thoughts included how her mother made her feel so special in presenting her with special gifts at times. Ali didn't want to lose in a track race. She was only in elementary school, and at the finish, she ran as fast as she could into her mother's arms, and Tamara scooped her up. A mother's love for her little girl was always there.

Taylor recalled how Tamara had talked to him in a baby voice: "I am Baby Huey. I am Baby Louie. I am Baby Dewey!" A mother playing tenderly with her boy.

Gentry recalled she and her mother being caught in a rainstorm. They tried to outrun it but got drenched. They laughed together, and she remembered the feeling of discovery and adventure.

The point is, everything was positive, nothing negative. Even Tamara's discipline, though strong, was because of devotion and love. They mentioned nothing about her death except that she died strong. I suppose that is why all three were so strong at the funeral. I recall how amazed I was. It was fitting and honorable. I felt I had little choice but to present myself in the same manner. I made sure her funeral was positive.

Of course, the time after her death wasn't always spent in positive realms. I suppose by the record, my son and I revealed it more than my daughters did. Most likely the girls had their share of pain, but to their individual credits, they never showed it. If they ever did, I don't recall it.

I know I had issues with anger and bitterness. It would seem my son did as well. I can't say for sure how much of his troubles related to his mother, but based on things I witnessed as well as conversations we had, I am confident it played a part. He was the oldest. Mothers and sons. Fathers and daughters. Many refer to the special bonds between these pairs. One parent simply cannot make up for the loss of the other.

Ali shared with me that she had never looked at her mother and me as a couple but as parents. That would have made sense at her tender age. The girls are married now, and Taylor has experienced relationships. Perhaps now at an older age and with experience they can appreciate how we in fact were a couple: two people married and committed to one another and the offspring we created. With their realization of this must come some element of understanding how difficult the loss of our partnership was to endure.

Tamara and I were a couple. As all of you who have had a relationship or are in one know, it isn't always easy. I came from a troubled background—not much peace and harmony. Certainly I wasn't taken very seriously in high school by girls. I was very small physically for my age. It was a miracle I could wrestle well. If only I had been held back a year. I was like the kid brother to most of the girls I was interested in. I did have a short-term

girlfriend, and it was innocent and ended with surprising maturity for our age, admitting we were much too
young. While other guys were shaving and proud of
their chest hairs, I was the small, hairless wonder. This
made the twenty-year high school reunion mighty fun:
going back with Tamara, who was so attractive and gracious enough to let me dance with whomever; having a
full head of hair when others were losing theirs and not
quite the lookers they once were. It was interesting how
many now-mature woman wanted to dance with me. My
old girlfriend and I argued in fun about who had broken up with whom first, hopefully with as much maturity as we shared twenty years before when the actual
break-up occurred.

I had a few rough years after high school. With my
mother's suicide and troubles I have previously shared,
my early twenties didn't result in any lasting relationships. I was a young man trying to find myself.

After the first year of medical school, I was at a café.
The waitress struck me with a vision of life with her. It
was my first time meeting Tamara. She was slightly taller
than I and very slender, with beautiful skin and legs. I
couldn't help but notice those in her shorts. I was young.
Her smile—her daughters have that, especially Gentry,
while Ali has her eyes. Taylor has that smile as well: a
smile to die for.

I left the little café and didn't say a word. I was shy,
much as I am now but for different reasons. I drove to a

department store. The next thing I knew I was shopping for something. I didn't know what. Then I saw it: this blue blouse, with a string attached to a ruffled collar and short sleeves. It looked like her to me. I can't say for sure why. It did, though, so I bought it. Back to the café I went. I asked to see her. I gave it to her and asked if she would kindly give me her number and go out with me. She didn't. I think she must have thought this action fairly strange. I suppose it was. So was I.

I do remember running into her again. It was at a local bar/lounge. Several of the medical students gathered there on weekends after studying. I didn't go much, but I was there on this occasion. Tamara was there after her shift at the café. I approached and talked to her for a while. This time she gave me her number. I left the bar thinking I had finally met the partner I had been looking for.

I remember like yesterday her apartment. The particular music. The strawberry cups and saucers. Her bicycle. The first kiss. My God! I knew right then. So tender. Love. Her lips. Passion! She left me wanting only more of that. I believed she felt the same.

My apartment was in better shape. She was in school, studying education, and I was in my second year of medical school. It wasn't long before we were living together. It was my plan to give us time and make certain there wasn't insanity involved. She shared that idea. We all know how close together love and insanity can be.

It wasn't long before her parents came to town. They were and are great people. They have religious beliefs. It didn't go over well that we were living together. Her father and I had the talk. Three months later, with the only suit I had and a new twenty-dollar dress, Tamara and I were in front of a minister getting married. We were both nervous, and I thought about running. This I shared with Gentry when she asked me what she should accept in a lover and relationship. I told her when she and her man share the following: When he tells her, if I don't keep you, I will spend the rest of my life wondering. Wondering where you are. Wondering how you are. Where you are. Who you are with. If you are well and doing all right. If you are happy. If you are in pain. My wonder will turn into worry. In other words, I have a choice. To stay right here, with you by my side, for as long as we have, or spend the rest of my life wondering, worrying. It just won't be worth it, all that time and anxiety. I'd better stay put.

That was it. That was all there was. So the choice to stay was made. Tamara and I stayed. We would have fourteen years.

Medical school was far from easy. I didn't have financial backing. It was all on borrowed money—not just the regular student lending, but the ugly stuff as well. They called it HEAL lending from Chase bank. I can assure you, with interest accumulating before one could graduate and make money, the loans were far from healing.

But it was what it took to get the job done for me. That and the army reserve pay. After graduation I had intern and residency pay. That, along with emergency hospital work, helped a great deal.

Tamara finished her education degree. However, we soon got educated really well. We were introduced to parenthood, blessed with a son followed by two daughters. We soon learned that once children come into your life, your life is changed forever. You certainly learn, if you are a good parent, what true love is. There is no time for selfish thinking. We had, until Tamara's death, a beautiful family. It was common for us to receive compliments everywhere we went. I tried to have that continue after she was gone. How does one do that?

During our educations, there was stress. Tamara and I struggled with religion. We tried to find a place we both could go and believe in the good of it. Every time we moved along my educational duties, we faced the religious dilemma of finding yet another church to attend.

Medical issues came up for us a few times. Tamara nearly died giving birth to our second child. Apparently, a retained placenta suggesting evidence of what could have been a twin caused significant blood loss. She survived. We had our moments of near death long before her cancer.

Yet there were many cards, flowers, and holding hands. Tamara and I watered the plants like our relationship so they as well as we could grow with love. For the most part, with the exception of a few quarrels, there wasn't much negativity. Certainly there was no drinking or adultery. I had learned to avoid that. I knew she was disappointed in me a few times along the way. I felt the same toward her on occasion. I maintained the thinking that overall we were blessed, and there was love. Solid love.

I remember a fellow student's spouse commenting to me at Tamara's funeral that she remembered that I gave my wife flowers at our medical school graduation instead of the other way around. She stated she was aware then of the love and respect we shared.

Despite this there were two occasions I believe I should share only because they reveal what I think true love is. It is when there is the ebb and flow of the tide. The point is that when storms come, you walk through them together and run if you have to. Whenever the end comes, your love is stronger and better than ever. Ours stood the test of the time. I am, of course, referring to death and not divorce.

I served my residency in Ohio. We were blessed to purchase a small, cute home for our family. It was our first. It turned out not so easy to unload when we left, but it sure was great to come home to at the end of the day while we were there.

I worked a lot. Between the weekend duties required and those I spent moonlighting and with the army reserve drills, no doubt I was busy. Tamara had her hands full with the kids. I look back and think perhaps the boxing I did was a selfish thing. I had something I wanted to prove to myself, but there really wasn't the time for it. I made the time. I forced it, I suppose. Tamara was against it, but I was stubborn about boxing. I ran to work, worked out over lunch, and ran home. Tamara would put the kids in the van a few times a week and follow me as I ran in the evenings. I had a heavy bag in the basement, so I didn't need to be away from home to hit that. It was the time involved to go to the fights, the time to find a gym and spar some. It was nuts. I was crazy. It went back to the time at the YMCA and my mother slapping me. Of course, getting the hell beat out of me the first few times didn't help. I am surprised it ended well and that my residency trainer even let me do it.

I came home one evening, and Tamara was gone. So were the children. I knew she was having a hard time adjusting, and this was the farthest she had ever been from home. I didn't support her with the loving kindness I should have. The night before, the kids and I had been on the couch watching *Lady and the Tramp* and *Winnie the Pooh* videos. Sometimes you can think things are OK, but they're not. You have to pay attention to the warning signs, such as coming home and finding your wife in a state of panic—obviously a time when love and patience are needed and mandated, really. Not the time for the Super Bowl halftime speech, which was what I gave.

After the panic of not knowing where my family was, and soon realizing suitcases were missing, I broke down and made the embarrassing call to her father in Iowa. He is one of the greatest men I have ever known. So he gave his daughter one night's sleep and sent her right back to me. It was a quick trip for her, but I had learned a big lesson. This marriage was to be a relationship, and there was no room for a bully. I admit I was angry. After I calmed down, I asked her what I needed to do. I didn't make demands. I asked for compromise. I will admit I asked her if I could finish boxing, since I had only two more fights. After the Golden Gloves, even if a miracle occurred and I won, I would take it no further. She reluctantly agreed.

In the end I was the one who nearly called it off. I called her dad and asked him if he thought I should continue. His advice was "You've come this far, taking a couple of beatings. If you don't fight in the Golden Gloves, win or lose, you will never know. Never lay to rest whether you could have done it or not. Go for it, son!"

I did, and I won. I know I wouldn't have without Tamara; Terry; Ted; my father-in-law, Norm; and my son, Taylor. My daughter Ali was too young to go, and Gentry wasn't born yet. She was in her mother's tummy at about six or seven months, I think. I won for them as well. I had talked to my father some. As I recall, he didn't have much to say. Our relationship was still on the mend from all that had happened, but as I indicated, with the help of my stepmom, that ended very well.

The other thing happened after my residency was complete. We were in Southern Missouri, and I had finally found the job Tamara and I had searched for— something that paid well and would give us the chance to pull ourselves out of debt. It also offered a good working environment and a decent place to raise children. Again, though, we faced the challenge of where to worship. This was very important to Tamara. It wasn't as much to me, and that was where trouble surfaced. We visited churches, but it didn't take me long to get fed up with religion. I just couldn't see my way past the man-made rules. I was interested in being spiritual rather than religious.

Within my frustration I found the obvious solution: give up and do neither. It seemed to me that each denomination had its strengths and weaknesses, all praying for one another for the error of the other's ways and claiming that the wrong interpretations of the Bible left us in danger of eternal hellfire. I couldn't get around this. I cried foul and laid claim to the idea that it was hopeless. Are we all bound for flames, after all the pain we deal with here? Tamara invited me to a spiritual retreat. I was not interested. She made sure I got interested, and off we went to be healed.

We got there, and in the room with all the other hopefuls, we were asked to grade our marriage and place the grade on a small piece of paper. Then we were to give the papers to each other and go back to our rooms and discuss the grades. We would start the official course the next morning. So we wrote, and then we went back to the room and gave the papers to each other. I was smiling, not wanting to seem vain. I tried to fake humility by giving us a slightly lower grade than what I believed. I handed Tamara our B plus. The smile was erased from my face quickly. She calmly and directly handed me my C minus.

I became furious! I thought, *Ungrateful...*I won't say what I thought, because I loved her, and that was only anger talking. I asked to leave. I said, "If this is the way you feel, then I am done!" Really, how did we deserve this? Truthfully, we came close to not making it to the next morning together, but I calmed down. I remembered the suitcases and Ohio. I owed her a lot. She was a wonderful mother, a great person. Not perfect, but certainly as good as I was. I had nothing on her. She deserved reason. She had stood by me through school and all the sleepless nights, the army, and the ER duties. Sure, she benefited, but she sacrificed. Three children she bore me. She was my woman. She deserved and had earned a chance to speak, and I needed to listen. I needed to figure this out. This is where many fail. They don't give or afford the other the chance—the chance to fix it, to make it work.

So I listened. It came down to the fact that I was not the spiritual leader she needed in the home. Despite the vacations we could take (not many), the flowers and cards, the sex and passion, the devoted parents, the date nights, there was still this void: This thing that was of vital importance to her. The key that would give us a chance at immortal love. Love that would continue after this life was over. The spiritual connection. It wasn't religion. It was spirituality. I took it on the chin like so many good punches I had endured.

We were there the next morning, ready to go. I gave it all I had. We left there committed, both in love, ready to reach for an A. We compromised. We made a deal that if we could stop looking for the perfect church, I would lead devotions at the house. I would pray before meals. I would read the word of God with her. We each kept our deals and found a place to worship. Our marriage grew and got stronger each day and week that passed.

I have fond memories of Tamara's desire to help anyone she could. Yet these memories are somewhat humorous as well. The problem was that Tamara had trouble finding people who could be helped or who desired help. I recall her getting out of the car once to approach a woman who appeared to be homeless and have everything she owned in a shopping cart. This resulted in Tamara being chased back to the car while the woman was trying to beat her over the head with something from the cart.

I asked, "How did that work out for you?" That didn't go over so well.

Then there was the time she brought a desperate soul home for dinner. This didn't end well. The person spat his food out and made several trips to the bathroom. The results of that left us cleaning for hours with bleach, masks, and gloves. After I took him home and returned, I asked Tamara if we might take a break from these efforts for a time, maybe think it through a little better. We laughed, got through it, and eventually had a couple of better experiences. To this day those memories bring a smile to my face.

Our debts were cleared. We took the kids to Disney World, and we took our trip to a tropical paradise. We decided to stay and build the home, and the rest of the story you know. How did we know cancer and death would be coming?

Oh my dear God, why? I asked this question when the cancer came to take my baby from me, the one I had grown with and learned to love unconditionally. I was able to look past the devastation of the disease and see the soul underneath, and before Tamara's last breath, I looked into her eyes, and I saw what she saw. I saw the best in me rather than settling for what I had been. I saw the gift she gave. I saw me at my best.

I loved her more than ever before. A tangled, paralyzed body. Broken spine and wearing a diaper, swollen from the steroids. It was going to be a closed coffin, but what I saw was the most beautiful woman in the world. My soul mate. The woman who challenged me to be better. Did I live to find anger again? Bitterness? Yes, I did.

Because I missed her. Because just when I figured it out, she was gone. She was taken. I made sure her last wishes were granted. All was done according to her will. That was when I found out I was a good actor. I performed well even though I was hurting badly inside. She wanted no anger. No negativity. She got it.

Tamara, please forgive me; I couldn't hold it forever. I suppose in doing this, I let the kids down some. Maybe you too. I just know now it is finally over. The anger is gone. It has been replaced by love. The children have seen it. It took a while. I made many mistakes, dear, but I did a few things right. You can see it in them. All of them now. I did try. Thank you for giving me the gift of true love.

If I am not ashamed of my believe in you then you have promised you won't be of me when my time here is over. Instead, thank you, God, or whatever any of you believe the higher power is. Just thanks. Thanks for the gift of time and love. Thanks for the chance to know what it was. What it is. What it isn't. Thanks for the dance. Thank you for the last kiss. It was different, of course, darling. It was more special than the first, which says a lot.

Thanks for demanding I be better, baby. That reminder brought me back around to a place where I can be of value again, a place of love. Oh, I know sometimes I will blow it, but not for long, baby. I am a better person for loving you, for losing you, and for it all. Better in some ways than I have ever been. It took me a while.

I am stubborn. I am here, though. I will see you again. It won't be long. For whatever time I am here, I will make a difference. I will die trying. I will swing with the knock-out punch I had. Only with love I pray.

The children are unaware, Tamara. They don't understand how we were tormented for a time with the idea that we were not each other's first choice, or our difficulties in coming to peace with that notion. They don't know the anxieties you endured over religion or being moved so far away from your home and parents. It was the medical training, Tamara. What was I to do? The moving around to find a place to pay off those hideous educational loans. After we did, how we struggled to decide whether to move or stay. What a difference only six months would have made if we had not built the home. What seemed to be the right thing to do at the time turned into the one thing we would have never done! And oh, the insanity that caused when I dwelt upon it! I never was able to speak to you about dying, Tamara. It wasn't spoken of out of respect for your fight to live. I had no opportunity to ask what you would want me to do afterward. Stay or go? There was only the mention of watching after our son. Everyone was so exhausted after you passed. I was at a loss to know how to carry on.

I remembered later the one option that for some reason never came to my mind until years later: the job I had been offered to teach at a medical school. A job not dependent on running a practice and insurance might have been just the correct formula for helping me be a single parent. Or I might have had the chance to meet someone more appropriate to help me with the children. Here I go again, looking back. This serves no purpose. We must strive to move forward.

I have lain awake at night, thinking of your voice, Tamara. My background with the piano. Ali's voice, inherited from you. The difference your life might have made in theirs and the choices I made. I have dreamed of your voice and Ali's, combined with Taylor and Gentry, who are accomplished in instruments: performances of peace and beauty replacing confusion or harsh realities. How great that would have been. All this and more. My haste in providing what I thought was more but perhaps merely less. Oh dear God, the torment of entering one's mind alone without the comfort of another!

In the end we knew we were each the one. The one we each had been looking for. Even though we did discover it before you became sick, how I loved you when you took your last breath. The look you gave me assured me of the pain you had in leaving me. Yet it gave me comfort in knowing you had selected the right man to finish the task you had started.

I don't think they know, Tamara. Maybe from my grief through the years, or the movie, possibly. Regardless, I loved you deeply. Thank you for helping me believe you felt the same toward me.

Despite Taylor's troubles, they all liked Texas, Tamara. They said so.

For those who have felt like this, the *love and loss*, I do understand. In this case again, you are not alone. It is love we lost, and love is the only thing that can heal the wound. Love is the only cure for the disease. It is by love and for love we continue on until that time finally arrives when with love we are allowed to share and spend eternity with the one we once loved so deeply.

In fairness, I think what someone told me over dinner is partially true: you will always love your wife, and there will never be another for you. Tamara was a hard act to follow for me. I did believe I had enough love left to try again. Fear of the pain of loss was part of it. Again, no love in that. I did try and, for reasons stated before, finding the right person at the right time didn't happen. I did experience the love of a woman in my life, though. I am thankful for that, even if it ended before I would have liked. It has been asked of me, "Do you feel you have lost your first or last love?" I pondered. Up to now it has most often seemed to be both. Presently in our society first loves are rarely the last. It does happen, though not as often as in previous generations. It is better to have your first be your last, I believe. For your last love is someone who did accept you despite what life threw at you both. If one has lost their first, there is love in believing in another chance to have a last love.

Bless you, Tamara, for sharing my heart and soul. I will be home soon. You'd better show me around. I am bad with directions.

Listen! For those who have lost: The love. The passion. The never-ending torment and loneliness. The shock of love being there and suddenly ripped away! The never-ending idea that love is gone forever. Empty arms. Lips that are dry, parched by the lack of another's touch. The search that finally came to an end only in a moment to begin again, to be involved in the madness of the chase for the validation that only love gives. You are not alone! The darkness and the feeling of being alone are present. Remember this! It took one defined moment to discover endless love. In the same brief unexpected moment, love can find you again. Your chances increase the more you give it! We are told it is better to give than receive. Oh, but for love. The untold leap of joy when the gift of giving turns on a dime, and love returns. The depth of appreciation made possible by the loss of love. Love is now so much more! Why? Because of the loss. Again pain teaches us to love. And love ends the pain. Love did find me again after decades. God's delay is not his denial. I discovered the warmth again provided by love and the conversations by the fire—the fire of love. I gave for decades. Now I am allowed to receive once again from time to time. Thank you for the warm blanket. For the opportunity not to enter the mind alone.

My friends, travelers, if this can happen to me, it can happen to anyone!

CHAPTER 19

FLESH

Love and lust do not abide together

When I looked in her eyes I saw what she saw.
The better part of me. The need to be better
rather than settle for what I had been. She was
my soul mate.

—*Between Heaven and Hell*

Death cannot stop true love. All it can do is
delay it for a while.

—*The Princess Bride*

As we travel through this life with the common
thread of a time to be born and a time to die, it
is my contention that the cure for regret, pain, loss,

mistakes, foolishness, selfish desires and thoughts, and a list of other negatives is love. The lyrics "If you want to get to heaven, you've got to raise a little hell"—Ozark Mountain Daredevils—makes more sense as one ages. Nothing grows without a little rain.

How many kingdoms have fallen and risen due to the powers of the flesh? My God, this challenge is a tough one. I am filled with agonizing memories. I have chosen to write about this along with all that has preceded it. Why? I am pouring out my life as blood on your doorstep. I am not holding back. No privacy here. Is it my epitaph? When I hit the last key, will I die? Will I be left to write more? Fiction or nonfiction? Stories to be remembered or forgotten? When my time has run out and I have to go, what can I leave behind? Surely my children are my legacy. Can my life count for something beyond that? Is my life an experience someone can relate to? How do we deal with life? The journey? What did it all mean for the so-called loser? The torn? The worn out? Those who feel there is nothing left?

In my case I am electing to share what I have experienced, to help us find something that can turn negative experiences around, make them meaningful and worthy of time, the outcome. Did we make fortunes? Die broke? Will we be recorded in history or be memories to die out in a generation or, at the most, two? Do we sum up our existence as something above the average or below? Is there a key that will unlock a door holding something that could last for an eternity? A life that touched so many and in turn the message within that life, spread by others, touching a thousand more? Millions? A message that continues to touch others long after the original spark ignited the fire? I believe there is. It is love! For those who know me or have known me, my children especially, this is me. This is what life dealt me. The good. The bad. The ugly. It is what it is. What you should remember is how I took it, how I played the cards. What did I learn? What did I return from what life gave? The same applies to you.

I was on my way home from basic training to pick up my car. It was a long bus ride. I was a very discouraged young man. My response to the events surrounding my mother's suicide was not good. *Bitter* is the only word that comes to mind. I was proud to wear the uniform but understood I was a college graduate unable to find a slot in officers' training school. At twenty-three I had two stripes on my sleeve. Far gone were the piano recitals with my mother's dream of me doing classical performances. There was no boxing career, no applause from the crowd as I fought for a championship that might allow my father to retire. Not only was he still working, but also drowning his sorrows with alcohol. I was a son going home. No trip to Hollywood. No movie. After all I had experienced, I suppose I thought the odds of my pulling that off were absurd. What was absurd, I now understand, was that I didn't try.

I stood at the bus stop, realizing it would be several hours before the next one arrived to take me home. A car approached. The driver asked if I had some time to kill. Kill was the appropriate word! I suppose it was the uniform and the naive look on my face. It was surely not the first time he had spotted a basic training graduate. He was not alone in the car. There was a good-looking young woman in the back seat. Again he asked if I had some time and money. I was not wise in the ways of the world but possibly not as innocent as he thought. I stood there considering all the possible outcomes. Truthfully, I did think it was a setup. I figured he would take me somewhere and have me beaten and robbed. What was unusual was that I didn't care. Not that my hormones weren't active. I cannot deny that. I was angry more than anything, however. I remember thinking, *Let's do it! Let it come!* I wanted to fight. Maybe I would get shot. Maybe I wouldn't. I would be able to get something in my hands. Let it come! Someone would go down with me. I would make sure of that. They had no idea what I was capable of. A young man outside of himself! Against the ropes of life. No clear thoughts. Just garbled nonsense. Anger. Bitterness. Pain. No love to be found. Nothing to offer neutrality. I knew I could fight, and why not? How we can pay dearly for moments of insanity, sober or drunk.

I got in the car, not caring where we were going. This was my life. This was how it would end. I was choosing this. No more piano lessons. No more religious hypocrisy. All right, God. There is no love here on earth. Who really gives a damn about anyone? I won't play for anyone to sing in church anymore. Let's just end this thing called life. It is overrated! All I want is to take someone with me. I can do that! I will do that!

As we were driving, I remembered standing outside a club a year earlier, watching a group of young men beat and kick another man senseless. The police eventually came, an ambulance also. It didn't look good. I couldn't imagine that young man living. Now it was my turn. I can't say what came over me. I know is there was no love involved. I was not scared. I was empty.

We pulled up to some old building, and the woman got out. I looked at the driver, and he asked if I had the money. I replied, "For what?" He indicated it was for her. It was all a bad joke! I said sure and got out of the car. I followed her as she opened the door to a room, and we went inside.

Once there I waited. I stood in a corner while she went to the bathroom for a moment. I don't remember thinking about anything. I was numb. Not a care in the world. Looking back, I have to ask, after all that I had known and all I had experienced, was this rock bottom? Perhaps at that moment it was. I lived on to have my share of worse heartaches. Other jagged rocks. Other greater depths. Agony and despair. This was most likely the poorest I handled tragedy up to that time. I was not able to see the light within the darkness. This could well have competed for the worst of me. I believe later in life, during the period I drank alcohol, I performed worse.

This wasn't about losing my virginity. That was already gone. It happened in college at the age of twenty-one. The experience took longer to occur than most. It wasn't positive, and I wept. I wanted it to be an expression of love. It wasn't. Things I had heard about but did not see in my parents relationship. The young college woman was horrified by my tears.

The event described here was about revenge. It was about wanting to get even. The irrationality was evident, but not to me. How was I getting even? With whom, with what?

The woman reappeared from the bathroom with nothing on but underclothing. I was still waiting, but no one else came. They never came. It was only her and me. I listened while she explained this was something she didn't do often. She needed money for shelter and food for her child. Reality came back to me. What had I done? Why was I here? Stupidity! My childhood and the parenting in my youth had left me very confused. Certainly love in all forms was one of them. Sex seemed dirty outside of love. It wasn't something I was ever well versed in. (If I am not honest here, there is no point in this writing.) Love was not involved in this case, which is evident. Many emotions were, but not love.

I conversed with her awhile. I was lonely and just out of confinement. I had temptation. Needs? Sure. But I also had a great deal of shame. I apologized to her. I

gave her money out of guilt. I did want to help her somehow. There was no desire to get her in trouble. I had
difficulty sexually. There was no satisfaction from the
act at all.

We walked back to the car. I gave the driver money,
hoping he wouldn't take too much of hers. He dropped
me off where he had picked me up. I waited again at
the bus station. The next ride I had was on the bus. At
least I can say I have never taken another ride like that
one. It was senseless—foolish and vain, showing no
respect for myself or anyone. No love or any merit were
expressed in this absurd notion. Nothing worse happened, which was fortunate indeed. A higher power
was looking out for me and without question wasn't
finished with me yet. One more event to be ashamed
of. Nothing was gained except the realization that I
never wanted to be part of anything like that again.
Youth and ignorance. At that moment I had disgraced
the uniform. I ask for forgiveness, for that more than
anything other than disgracing God, myself, and the
woman.

I do feel it's appropriate to mention something that
has been asked of me on occasion. What is more honest or less damaging, if not cheaper: a marriage based
on nothing more than money, gaining citizenship, or
some advantage not otherwise obtainable; or simply
paying for sex as an exchange for what some believe is
a natural need, a physical requirement to be healthy? I
think for some, this type of relationship may work to a

degree. Those involved in such can't care much. If they do, someone will get hurt.

I have expressed that marriages or commitments based on the above will fail at some point. They typically do. Once the temporary need is met, nothing else is left. The need is there, but the marriage is only a temporary fix that fades to nothing over time. The greater need, truthfully, is not met, for love isn't involved. Rather, the need is for love. People, I believe, fool themselves into thinking they don't need love. I believe love is the need. Nothing but boredom remains after the lack of meaning or love. This leads to separation and divorce most of the time, not to mention the lack of even a physical attraction due to an age difference or lack of respect.

On occasion it does work, I think because the people involved fall in love, or at least a form of it. They at least develop a deep respect for each other. For those who commit to marriage, this bond should represent respect, honor, and integrity. Others look at it as only a contract. It's not needed, and they would rather be together because they want to rather than feel forced. Why? The rationale and point are clear. Without love, all is meaningless, marriage or not. The hot-blooded sex can dissipate over time. The lasting encounter is fed by undying love.

My answer is that in the long run, without love you have nothing at all. I cannot argue, however, that the exchange spoken of perhaps would be cheaper depending on several factors, one of which is that you do not catch an incurable disease. Also, outside of only a few places, prostitution is illegal. Regardless, relationships that are shallow and void of any true meaning and have nothing to do with love don't work out well. Actions void of love simply lead to trouble the majority of the time. Many people who have done horrible things have attributed their deeds to a lack of love.

Is it possible for two consenting adults to enter into a physical relationship to satisfy so-called needs and leave it at that? I have been told this is so. It certainly hasn't worked out that way for me. At some point, it seems, there is an effort by one party or the other to take it to another level, one of deeper meaning, requiring at least a basic level of respect. In other words, this basic need many times doesn't turn out to be that basic. It becomes more involved. I maintain that is because the need, truthfully, is greater—the need to be loved and cared for. For the human who has not become entirely selfish, there is the need to return the love that is given.

Nothing is free. I believe each of us as humans has a need to be loved, and at least most have the need to return it. Perhaps not everyone. When a person doesn't care about love, not giving or receiving it, I maintain, peace is not in his or her heart. It has been replaced with some inner conflict involving hatred or bitterness. These are generally not kind people. As mentioned before, they are narcissists, people best left alone until they can find ways to love and be loved. You may, of course, try to reach them and help them find their way. That is love. Over time, however, if you fail and are fatiguing badly, it's better to give to another who can receive and give back. Initially, love isn't conditional on receiving love in return, but it will be eventually. I see nothing, nor have I read anything, that indicates love in its true form should make one deathly ill. Giving love without receiving any back and accepting that means you do not love or respect yourself.

I lived with a true love. I had it, and I lost it. I tried and failed to find another for a long time. Love must be given space if one is to have it again. I didn't get it done. Maybe I got what I deserved. Maybe not. What do we deserve? What do we get? What do we choose? With open heart a new and last love can find you and you it once again! Some may choose to live life alone after the loss of love on this earth, at least regarding a romantic love and bond with another. Even so, don't lose the opportunity to give love to others. In doing so you may lose yourself.

It was hard to write about this, hard to share. I ask my daughters to forgive me. I attempted to teach them better, their friends as well. I had to struggle through anger and bitterness. I would like to think that with all the love I shared, I did better, as time went on, around the fences of pain and loss. To all those I have loved or tried to love and failed, I ask for your forgiveness. If I failed you, believe me, I also failed myself.

Son, I suppose you know now why I hung in for so long. Why I couldn't give up: my understanding of the heartache, the bitterness, the foolishness, the reckless abandon. Son, I've always loved you, through it all. I suppose it is true that what goes around comes around. Forgive me, son. This time love will conquer the pain. You will see to it. I believe that.

David and Bathsheba. Samson and Delilah. Helen of Troy. It is long list: faithless love and the cheaters who have come and gone through years of endless tears. The centuries of wars and the rumors of it. How much pain created from the desire of flesh?

Is it a natural desire? Certainly there has to be truth in that. This ensures the continuation of humanity. Can it go wrong? Is there a divine purpose for that contact between a man and a woman? An expression of kindred spirit? A togetherness not shared with all? A special bond?

Is there no shame? No terms of enduring love? For those I have loved and loved true, there is no harm, no foul. When it didn't work, I take my part of the blame: For the cheated. The one night of an absurd notion. The times when heart was not there, not from one or the other. For me, my part, I ask for forgiveness. I ask for what was missing. Love. It is love that is the truth. It can and will erase all fouls: the stench of immorality, the pain of life. Remember one thing: when all else fails, there is love. It remains.

Thank you, Eric Clapton, for writing the following words in "River of Tears":

It's three miles to the river
That would carry me away
Two miles to the dusty street
That I saw you on today

It's four miles to my lonely room
Where I will hide my face
And about half a mile to the downtown bar
That I ran from in disgrace.

Lord how long have I got to keep on running?
Seven hours, seven days, or seven years?

All I know is since you've been gone
I feel like I'm drowning in a river
Drowning in a river of tears.

I wish that I could hold you
One more time to ease the pain.

This will save me. This can save us all. This and only this. The *gift*. The gift of love.

I have shared the embarrassments. The depths of pain. How they formed me. How they started. The choices I made as a result of pain. The results of those choices.

Why? I cannot be alone. There must be others who have made poor choices and had to live with them. The hurt. The bitterness. Actions taken as a result that only served to make it worse. Cast your burdens on a higher power and not on yourself—that's the teaching. Do not lose faith or purpose. This is not easily done. This mechanism of believing and trusting in a higher and more noble truth certainly can be a great foundation for love. It also provides a formula to reduce the heartaches and not create more.

If I allow myself to return in my mind to the bus station, this is what I think of. The woman and I would not even recognize each other now. I couldn't have identified her a few days later back then. If I could stand in front of her, though, what would I do? What should I do? Ask for forgiveness, of course. Ask her if she found love or if it found her. Ask if she is well, if she had found a way into the light from the darkness. Then ask myself the same and demand better of myself. I did. I have. You can as well.

I am sorry. I am ashamed. However, there is no love in that. I was sorry. I was ashamed. Love has erased it. I am reminded only not to do it again.

There may be those who disagree. I am not in judgment of you, for I am guilty at least of trying the same. Sex would on the surface seem to be a need there is no harm in fulfilling as long as both parties understand. However, I can bear witness and have discussed with many others that sex without love tends to create and lead to pain more often than not. There is no other truth than this. When love attempts to enter, these vain and superficial connections fade quickly because love reveals the superficial act of sex for what it is. There is no love in it, so love cannot abide there.

Since love is the only enduring, everlasting truth, do not be surprised when any relationship without love is nothing more than faded memories and reminders of why you are alone now, regarding the physical—because you flirted with love and in doing so lost it. One can tease life and love and be left empty. There's nothing to do but pay for yesterday when love asked of us and we denied it. Please ask of yourself. Do not say no to love!

Do not let your pride, ego, and vanity negate the need to be ashamed. Do not live in shame, for there is no love in it! Let the mistakes go! Why? Because they negate the knowledge you gained. Relationships are not easy, as can be attested to by the massive numbers of divorces and bitter endings. Yet relationships are so easy—those founded and watered by the love that accompanies mercy and reward, the reward of never-ending lust created by the passion of two souls that become one. Hold on for this, for I know no love deeper. The depth of the ocean cannot compete!

CHAPTER 20

RACISM
All blood is red

*Passion makes the world go round. Love just
makes it a safer place.*

—Ice T

There have been many books written lately on thinking positive, believing in the positive. The sugges-
tion is you can make demands of the universe and,
given enough positive energy, turn things around. It
has been referred to as the great secret: Make good
things happen. Have abundant life. There must be an
element of truth in it. However, I also believe that much
of it is a great lie! Negativity certainly doesn't make for
a better life: Drowning in sorrow. Crying out the woes
and saying, "Poor, pitiful me!" Do that long enough and

see how many friends you have, how many people want to hang around to see the bleeding wounds. Yet I can remember a decade or more ago, when other writings were published, things such as *When God Doesn't Make Sense*. These were great works. As I recall, many copies were sold. I can say this: We live in the world. Night falls here. To believe that positive thinking results in only positive things is not realistic. We are imperfect. So is the world in which we live. The key is to take the trials and tribulations and turn them around, make them work for you rather than against you.

I believe this is the answer in this life, where confusion, sense, love, and hatred all coexist on a daily basis: Find a middle ground, a place to stand. Be realistic about life yet inspire those around you. Find a place of quiet rest where one can let God be supreme, let the universe be the unknown. Realize that things happen to us no matter what we might be thinking at the time. Understand that our duty lies in the way we deal with such things. Refuse to stop loving. Quit hating. I am making an effort to do so and inviting you to come along for the ride.

Racism: I cannot understand this. I truthfully can't. I get that we grow up differently in this country or another. I comprehend that humanity has cultural differences. In the end, though, don't all of us have a common thread? A time to be born? A time to die? When we bleed, the color is red—red for us all. Why can't we just be humans, here together, trying to help one another along the way? Why the hatred? The shootings? The inflicted pain? The evil? The negativity? What does it accomplish? What is the great end?

What did Hitler and those like him ever prove? What is his legacy other than death, fear, terror, and torture? When his end came, what was his conclusion on the matter? To take his own life. That's how it ended. There was celebration that the reign of hatred and horror had ended. This man. His life. His breath. All of it had ended. What kind of legacy is that? Madness!

He is only one, but my God, there have been so many. One could pen a thousand chapters and not have covered them all. I will not try.

I was born in the South and raised in the North. I visited the East and longed to see the West, the romantic West. How many Westerns have I watched? I think every one ever made. There's a hero. The good. The bad. The ugly. Most of the time, the good wins out. That's the romantic notion. I like those movies. Justice is swift and fast. Truth wins out. People get what it seems they have earned. At least that is what I have observed.

I have not traced my family history. I do know Faulkner came from Falconer. At some point we trained birds for the nobles. I've always liked birds. Maybe that is in my blood. Maybe it's why I accepted being shit on sometimes. Ha!

I never wanted to know about the Civil War, though, as far as which side my ancestors fought on. Maybe both sides. I understand there were political issues and economic concerns. No matter. I never wanted to know if anyone related to me had anything to do with the slavery of another human. I honestly didn't want to know that. The entire process sickens me. I can take solace in knowing that members of my so-called race did fight and die standing against it.

History is history. All we can do as humans, I think, is learn from it. All I can do is voice my opinion. I was never proud of the Confederate flag. Please understand that I acknowledge it doesn't represent for some the same things it does for others. For me it is a reminder that this country was divided. Many lives were given and lost. In the midst of it, there was a race of human beings who stood between the right to live free or not. That is very sobering for me, very painful. I am glad it is over. At least it is supposed to be. This hatred. This hypocrisy. There is the admission, from what I can see, that many do not wish to ever let it go. Though there is not supposed to be a side anymore, I am thankful I lived to see a day when that flag was placed in a museum and not flown or celebrated as much. We serve the stripes, what they stand for, or at least what they are meant to stand for.

For those who wear outfits of white and call for supremacy; those in inner-city black gangs who murder and view life with hatred; those who believe in using ugly words to describe other races; those who commit acts of terror: What does any of this have to do with love? What are you changing for the greater good by killing and taking the head off of another human—by doing this to someone who has not taken an innocent life, someone who has not assaulted or mutilated, an innocent victim of your hatred? What kind of heaven are you going to? A heaven that celebrates this? A universe that will give you a reward? Help us! What kind of place can that be?

I ask, please stop! Just stop. Put the hatred down. Pick love up. Find that and embrace it. Don't live your life like this. Maybe hating is easier than finding a reason to love. If we as humans are lazy, then perhaps that is our greatest offense, to take the easier way out. It is nothing less than fear—the fear that keeps us from casting mere shadows rather than living boldly with courage and helping others do the same. When you look at me, don't see white. I ask you to be color blind. I will for you. You have my word.

If you still wear or have a swastika, what does it represent? Is it love or hate? Are you making a statement? Is it a good one or not? Ask yourself and make a choice, a choice that represents love.

Through the centuries we have been great about this, haven't we? Hating. Greedy for land and power. Imposing our wills upon others. It happens globally. It happens in the home, between spouses, parents and children, and siblings.

As humans we are quick to judge, to find fault. Excuses are better than reasons. I understand there are times when one is left in the cold of bitterness and pain. When the time comes to react, what was gained by adding another insult, another regret, another stained memory?

I was mugged. I was kicked and slapped around by both white and black gangs as a youth. I remembered the hate, the prejudice. It was good that I could run fast. Very good. Yet it was members of the so-called black race who were my best and dearest friends when serving in the armed forces. Thank God I never ended up in a foxhole or in war. But if I had, it would have been a blessing to have them there.

I see no more sense in racism than I do in "partisan" activities. Where did this strong division come from? Not the ideas of a human being but rather a platform. That's a great word to use: a *platform*. Something to jump off of. Perhaps our leaders could do us a greater good by jumping. At least for once they would all be together.

The presidential race prior to Mr. Trump winning was about as ugly and childish as anything I have witnessed. I pray for a return to honor, integrity, and love. The world needs that. The world needs us. All of us. I have never claimed a political party. I always look at the individual. Party divisions seem to accomplish little other than creating the intense desire to remain divided.

Divided we fall. Together we stand. How I relish the principled idea that leaders would humble themselves enough to sincerely apologize for wrongs, to ask for forgiveness, and then move forward, expressing the values and beliefs they stand for—what they offer without the continual beating on the failures of another. Clean it up. Stand firm, yet love.

This is a mere chapter. Entire books have been written on this. In the end, it is simple. Love is far better than hate. It is. It always will be. How does one answer the hard questions? How do you explain people who cried for unity in the name of love and mercy yet died violent deaths? To attempt naming all of them, of course, would mean to leave many out. I won't try. Yet whether your faith says that Christ was a good man, a prophet like others, or the son or one of the sons of a living god, was he crucified? Millions have been taught so. What did he do besides teach love? Forgiveness? Mercy? What did he indicate was the greatest command? Love, of course.

I cannot possibly do justice to all those who taught that love is greater yet died violently. Martin Luther King Jr. certainly gave his life trying to stop racism. I personally think he would be disappointed to see it continue. It's interesting that Abe Lincoln gave his life for a reason similar to King's, a man from a different race. Race? It is so very discouraging to see our leaders and general population today continuing to talk about it, keep making it relevant. Why can't we let it go? Let it die? Work together? Love one another?

Back to the Westerns and my time of giving thought to becoming a Texas Ranger. In the old days a swift and righteous judgment to the evildoer. Wanted dead or alive. Is one as good as the other? A part of me likes that, not to take a life for the humor of it. Rather to take revenge on the evil and wrongdoing of another. It's not a hard idea for most of us to come to. After all, how do you love those who have committed such evil? How can you, after what they did? So we lock them away. With their insanity and the life they have taken, what choice do we have? Can we allow them to take more lives? Should we put them to death? That's a matter of debate with careful regard and concern. Although we cannot love what they have done, we must love what they could have been.

Oh God, please forgive me for what I would want to do to someone who would punish, torture, and murder one of my children or my friends. Where would my so-called love be then? With all I have already endured in this life and journey, I cannot say. There is no need to ruin all I have penned with hypocrisy. All I could do is cry out for mercy and some limited understanding should that ever happen.

In the movie *Once upon a Time in the West*, there is an exchange I will never forget. A wanted man is being turned in for a $5,000 reward:

"Judas was satisfied with four thousand nine hundred and seventy dollars less."

"There weren't no dollars in them days!"

"But sons of bitches? Yeah."

A negative! Is it true they will always be here? One places faith in another life, one without all this hate. I would like to believe we could together try for better in this place between heaven and hell.

It is said it is better to have loved and lost than not to have loved at all. I believe this is true. I have done it. I would rather have had the love than to never have had it at all. I admit there have been times I have questioned it. Thanks, Mom, for the times you sang to me as a child and loved me, despite the awful things that followed. Thanks, my wife, for loving me despite the horrible ending. Thanks for your love, my children, despite the difficulties and tribulations. Thank you, family and friends, for all the love. Thank you. It felt very good. It still does.

Thanks to all who have suffered yet still chose to remain true to love. Thanks to those who gave up their lives for love. They certainly believed in it. They were put to the test. A decision was made: A choice. Something to leave behind. A legacy. It was love. As hard as it might be. As tough as the reasons not to. If one can hang on to something of value, something everlasting, it must be love! I am hanging on. I hope to continue.

Ironically, just as I hit the key for my last thought on this matter, I decided to view the news. Recently a city in the South decided, after ongoing racial tensions and a deadly shooting in a black congregational church, to remove the Confederate flag from its courthouse. A good idea and long overdue, in my opinion. Unfortunately, this did not occur without further incident. There was a protest march by a white supremacist group with a representative from the Ku Klux Klan, someone also showed up with a Nazi swastika. This group lined up against a black educators' group, and the result was violence that mandated police involvement. There was a picture of a black officer protecting the Klan member with the Confederate flag. How ironic!

Here is the irony. The Klan member admitted the events surrounding the Civil War were wrong. He still maintained that he had the right to preserve the flag and honor its place in history and those who died for it. All right. If I understand that correctly, then placing the flag in a museum of history would be appropriate. What is gained by publicly marching it through the streets and continuing to promote arguments and violence? Why? What's the point?

If forgiveness and love are ever to become predominant themes in this world, how can we let this continue? Why do we wait for someone to be murdered before a gang member can be arrested?

Gangs promote violence and death. Memberships promote division and racism. Some religions embrace murder. If I had my way, memberships to such groups would simply be illegal. They are a crime against humanity. They should be punishable by arrest and confinement until the person is willing to revoke his or her membership. I suppose that will never be, and this hatred will always be with us in this world. Actions that attack that principles of our nation would not be free.

Rather, they would be crimes against dignity and truth, crimes against compassion and freedom expressed in the form of love.

I do understand that hatred has no part in love. Love would command different. Please, brothers and sisters. Because we bleed red. All of us. Stop this. Ask yourself to love. Murder and rape are not love. Let love allow you to choose differently.

If you desire to continue this cause for the perpetuation of racism in any form and teach it to your children, I can only pray you stop, that you replace it with the love God intended you to give. Racism in any form is ugly, ignorant, and unjustified. Though hatred and the lack of love will forever be a part of this world, at least do your part. Take no part in it!

I am now going to give you choices. Let's say you're white. As a youth, you are beaten and robbed by a black gang. Your mother, nursing your wounds, throws out racial slurs. Your father comes home and in anger reinforces the idea that blacks cannot be trusted. Another racial slur is uttered. Through fear you become a covert racist. Your grow up with this experience imprinted in your memory bank. Decades later you experience a heart attack. Once you are in the emergency room and your diagnostic work-up is complete, you are told you need emergency cardiac bypass surgery. Without hesitation the ER physician tells you that the number-one heart surgeon in the region is available. He is black. It's your choice. Do you choose him or because you are a covert racist ask for someone else?

Your grandfather served in World War II. He was captured and held in a Japanese prison camp. Daily he was beaten and tortured in unimaginable ways. After he was freed and returned home, every day you spent with him he explained why he hated all Asians. When he saw one, he either became very quiet or uttered a racial slur. Being young and impressionable, and admiring your grandfather, you unknowingly become a covert racist. Despite your father and mother not speaking of this, it is held in your memory bank. In college you meet and fall deeply in love with an Asian woman. With some hesitation you tell your parents. You are shocked when for the first time they tell you this woman will never be accepted into the family. Both parents insist that you stick to your own race and religion and only consider a white Irish Catholic. You are reminded of your grandfather. Your parents let you know he will never speak to you again should you insist to continue your current relationship. You now realize that your parents have been covert racists but chose not to speak of it. You yourself also were one because when you first met the young woman, you were hesitant to ask her out. Your love for her overcame the impressions imprinted within. Do you now follow the love in your heart, desiring to have what you believe will be a beautiful life with her? Or, due to the racism of the family break her heart as well as yours while you look for someone you may not be in love with at all? Do you spend the rest of your life thinking about the love you gave up, which would result in strong resentment toward your family for the duration?

You have recently found out that your daughter has been raped and beaten by a Mexican man. Immediately you wanted to take justice into your own hands, but through restraint and understanding that you would end up in prison yourself, you decided that your daughter needed you more than ever, and you allowed the justice system to prevail. You never believed prior to this that you were racist. The media attention on illegal immigration and the political position that criminals are crossing the border by the thousands had been imprinted on your mind. You realized this when you asked the police if the accused was an illegal alien. It turned out that he was not, but your thoughts made this almost impossible for you to believe. When you understood that the defense attorney was making a sustained effort to have the jury be majority Mexican, you became infuriated. Naturally the prosecution was doing the opposite, attempting to assure the jury was majority white. Despite the fact that all minority jurors found the assailant guilty while one white sympathizer held out, causing the prosecution to move for a lesser sentence, you instructed your daughter to never trust another Mexican for the reminder of her life. And you made a choice not to ever speak to another Mexican or have anything to do with any for the reminder of your life.

Of course all of the above scenarios are interchangeable regarding race.

Thus ignorance prevails. Only upon admission of this covert tendency can we deal openly with it. To admit that this thought pattern exists is our only hope of curing the disease of racism.

I state again, the opening of mind and heart with the healing only love can provide is in fact our only chance for a cure! Let love guide you in a solid effort to let the covert go! Again take no part in it! This is not love!

CHAPTER 21

INTEGRITY

Words only matter when kept

Darkness cannot drive out darkness;
only light can do that.
Hate cannot drive out hate;
only love can do that.

—*Martin Luther King Jr.*

For me to pen this letter to God without brutal honesty, I believe, would be hypocritical at best. I would like to think this book is different from many others. Books have been written, both fiction and nonfiction. This is certainly not fiction. Most writers select topics of interest and then apply their respective talents to discuss what they have learned about them, what they may have studied regarding them. Others may have researched these topics as well. Some have shared experiences gained from patients or clients during counseling. There have been memoirs penned by those thought of as famous or having notoriety.

Mine is a human-interest story. I am a commoner laying out everything regarding himself. All of it. The good. The bad. The ugly. Why? Again I say, to help others. To sum things up. To ask the difficult questions of ourselves. The why and what for. To address the accountability. What have you given? What have you taken? What will you be remembered for? Where do you believe you are going after this life?

If I am guilty of anything in penning this, it may be that I shared too much. Some may say it would have been better left private. I made a choice not to do that but instead to express to you and myself the frailty of life, how difficult the journey can be and how much more difficult we can make it. I ask you to remember that this book is a letter not only to you but to a higher power. I suppose it can be looked at as a great confession. Yet the intent is for it to be more. I let you as the reader know me in a very intimate way. The memoirs of others—how much did they leave out? I want people to experience life changes. So I give myself up. As the crucified, I want my life to help you with yours.

I will turn a page now to the positives. I have done many good things, stood for many decent things through the years, and ministered to many patients.

They trusted me, and I have the letters, cards, and gifts to prove it. I gave. I was also honest enough to admit that at times I had been no better than any of them regarding poor choices. I had my problems in and with life as well. Because of this admission, I maintain, people and patients believed I was real, that what they saw was what they got. For better or worse, they at least knew where they stood, and before them was an honest person. I admitted mistakes. I reacted to tragedy and pain poorly at times. At other times I stood in the face of adversity with strength—mostly, I think, when I had the sense to lean on a higher power.

I believe I wrote this book with a degree of integrity despite my admission of not always practicing it. At times I've been far from it. At the least the confession has merit. I did attempt to always keep my word and do what I said I would do. To keep promises. Did I ever fail? It would seem so. Maybe it wasn't so much the breaking of my word but rather my poor reactions to pain. At the least I did break promises to God in not keeping his laws. Not that I excuse myself by feeling neglected by this higher power. I can assure you my intentions in life were above the mark. When I failed and reacted to hardships with resentment and bitterness, the results led to further embarrassment and more pain.

What of integrity? Why is this such a rare find in life today? Is it? It certainly would seem so. Honesty and goodness, mercy—these qualities are needed so much.

So is doing what you say you will do. The day of keeping promises and vows has faded into a muck of mud. Business partners who fail to perform. Friends who are our so-called best until they may be hurt. God forbid it might cost them some money or time.

Divorce is common. Legal needs have risen dramatically both for the plaintiff and the defendant. What is the common theme? Someone couldn't bear to keep his or her word. Unethical behavior. Broken agreements and hearts.

Why do people abuse poor, defenseless animals? The shelters are full of them. No need to ask about that, though; all over the world people are taking the lives of others, raping and molesting other humans. Parents? Just because two people were there to make "love" and create life doesn't make them good parents. Countless "parents" do everything not to pay for the support of those they brought into the world. In fact, their actions prove there was no binding love in their relationship.

My dad told me, "If you come to the end of your life and can count your true friends on one hand, you have been a blessed man!" He also let me know, "Son, you love deeply. This will cause *pain* and remorse. Why? Because seldom will this type of deep and committed love be returned to you. I have now lived long enough to believe what I once considered cynical to have an element of truth. He was partially correct. I did get hurt and still do. I did, however, experience the love of a woman. The love of my children. Books have been written on integrity. There is a tremendous need for in it in this world on all levels. Politics. Diplomacy. Whatever happened to good old Honest Abe? From global affairs to our jobs. The relationship between employer and employee. Between spouses. Parents. Children. What do we have without integrity and honor? Not much. All the money in the world cannot grant us these qualities. There is hardly any truth regarding the news. Only political favor. I recently visited our nation's capital with my younger daughter, Gentry. I had not been there for fifty years. I stood with her on the steps of the Lincoln Memorial, where I had stood with my father fifty years earlier. My words to her at the time were spoken with tears. I told her if I had known what the fifty years were to bring from then till now I doubt I would have had the courage to continue. The Capitol building. The White House. The Washington Monument, World War memorials, Vietnam memorial and others. It's not hard to see how we are still the greatest country on earth. The collective words of these men inscribed on the monuments and memorials: Truman, Eisenhower, Roosevelt, Lincoln, MacArthur, and a few others. My God! The honor! The respect! The integrity! What has happened? May God help us!

I maintain I loved Tamara. I love my children. Did I most often keep my word? Yes, I did for sure. I cared for my friends. I loved again after Tamara. The question is, Did I always approach life with integrity, without compromise? Truth without some sort of lie? Walking in the light without hiding in darkness? These are sobering thoughts. The answer is no, if for no other reason than the lack of acceptance regarding the tragedies. The lack of faith. Pain that was allowed to produce more pain. I made choices. I made a movie about them, *Between Heaven and Hell. The choices we make are the only thing we own.*

Tamara, I love you still. Children, I love you. I cannot measure the universe. Those who walked on the moon—what they must have thought looking upon the planet Earth and the universe beyond. I believe my love reaches the universe. Yet I have sinned. I have been financially and, more importantly, morally bankrupt. I have seen enough of hell that I desire not to abide in it. There have been times I have shown a lack of integrity. The sad thing is, I have known others who were at one time close to me, but their lack of integrity, by all available measuring, does certainly seem to dramatically exceed mine. My good God! That is terrible indeed.

I say again, for the sinner and the saint, for the faithful majority and the faithless minority, believing in the power of love can make the difference. For those with regret. For the punch drunk. The pain ridden. The times we looked in the mirror at ourselves and got sick. The miserable. The faint of heart. Those without courage left. There is the great eraser: love.

Get back up. Forgive others. Forgive yourself. Be thankful for the hard lessons. Be better. Stronger. Wiser.

Let the down times be fewer and shorter in duration. When all else is lost, when there seems no reason to go on another day, reach up. Ask for help from a higher power. Dust yourself off. Someone needs you. Someone needs your love. Regain your integrity. Do yourself and the world a favor: show another earth traveler some love. You will hurt less and have fewer regrets. There are no do-overs.

No one is saying not to be a little wiser. You don't have to return to the empty well that has caused so much pain. Yet you can still choose to love. There can be no integrity without knowing love.

I am not completely ignorant. At least I hope not. I have enough reason to comprehend insanity. There are those in this world who refuse to practice love or have anything to do with it. They murder and take lives. We live in an age of terrorism. Nations of innocent people are being brutally murdered. Our own nation is under attack. How does one extend love to that? There have been wars. I suppose on this planet, there will be always an element of hatred. It has to be dealt with as well: precisely, deliberately destroyed!

It is a shame, though. A shame that for some, love doesn't seem a possibility but, rather, an idea. It is our duty to love. Some have been programmed to hate and confuse that with love. They have been brainwashed with a disease of serving hate and death. It is for us and far better that we respect and care about life. Choosing love as much as humanly possible is the greater good. If we are called to end this insanity by taking life, let us do so with what mercy we can afford. Do it quickly, and do not take part in torture. Don't be like them despite the temptation to do so. Just end it. Do it in the name of love, even if this form is surely what is meant by tough love.

Mean what you say. Say what you mean. For yourself. For humanity. For the universe and the god that governs it. Love is the only real freedom you will ever have if it is given truthfully and with integrity.

Vince Gill had it right in his song "Whenever You Come Around": "The face of an angel; pretty eyes that shine / standing here holding the biggest heartache in town / and when you smile the world turns upside down, whenever you come around."

Love can do that—turn everything upside down. Without it, hope for anything to be right side up is lost!

CHAPTER 22

EPITAPH
Home at last!

Love is the voice under all silences,
the hope which has no opposite in fear;
the strength so strong mere force is feebleness:
the truth more first than sun,
more last than star.

—E. E. Cummings

I believe in a higher power. I realize this power is thought of in many different ways by several faiths and religions. The human race seems to have developed countless ways to find a method of reaching out to this higher good. Countless doctrines. Beliefs that at times seem to promote more fear than freedom. The development of many roads to hell rather than love. As if this earth and all the hatred toward humanity that is displayed in so many horrific ways are not hell enough.

I was frightened as a youth regarding religion. Quite frankly, I ended up more confused than anything else. The different beliefs among the Christian doctrines are staggering: topics regarding the day of worship, baptism, and so on, not to mention the many differences regarding the interpretations of what I was taught was the holy word of God, the Bible. One of the most interesting classes I took in college was the history of religion. For the first time outside my sheltered world, I was exposed to the teachings of Buddhism, Hinduism, Islam, and others. I recall comparing my Christian principles, questioning how many so-called principles I had been taught were rules or regulations to abide by or suffer the consequences. How much did these religious laws teach about love?

I did find there was a common thread among all of these different faiths, at least in their modern teachings. In ideal form they are all about peace, harmony, faith, and a connection to a higher power. Each is reaching out for understanding and a level playing ground, for hope of something better in another place. Each has a different holy book and serves a different prophet or son of God. They have different views on who Christ was or perhaps believe in another prophet. Yet the familiar themes are there: A universe. A higher power. A common good. Love. I could not see the bad in that. The principal of love taught in each belief.

How do we control where we are born? What we are taught? It should remain obvious to the intellectual as well as the so-called ignorant that love is good. Hatred is evil. That principle is just not that hard to grasp. Some Christians may look at this and say, "Well, now you're turning away from the one and only Christ!" I didn't say that. I have my beliefs, things that have been ingrained within me since birth. The same, however, must exist for others, and as long as their teachings embrace hope, peace, love, and respect for human life, why can't we work together? Belief systems that embrace the ideology that killing gives people some special entrance into a higher place of glory and special considerations surely have nothing to do with love. In them there is no respect for life. No integrity. How can one believe in a merciful god and practice that type of doctrine? My fellow travelers, if that is true, we are all in severe trouble. If that is the powerful energy we serve, then after this life, we are all bound for an eternal and unimaginable hell.

I shared my childhood that framed me, the growing pains that developed me. In many cases the examples of love and mercy were as clear as mud. There was love, although at times it was rather twisted. There was *pain*—enough of it to stir up negativity, bitterness, rejection, and anger. These roots of poison led to choices. When the choices were poor, they created more pain and negativity, an endless web of confusion and the wisdom of a fool.

Like the fighter in the ring, I countered. I regained composure and offered my family better. Forgave and asked for forgiveness. Gave mercy while asking for the same. Made sure my marriage was better than that of my parents, that the children were exposed to a stronger love and nights of peace. For years I stood as a rock and allowed no impurity or lack of integrity in our home. This peace I allowed to be taken from me. Death and destruction found me again and lay at my feet. Hurt and torn, I rebounded again from a few poor choices and regathered myself. I leaned against the ropes and fought back. I countered for the children and the memory of the woman I loved. Gave to the patients in need and shared love again to the best of my ability, though I was shaken. I knew I was frightened, not the rock I once had been, but still standing. In or out of the ring, I understood, there would be no medals for cowardice.

The military. Boxing. Medical school. Tough? Hardly. Single parenting? Now you're talking! But I got through it. At times was it harsh? I suppose so, given my struggle, but without a doubt, love remained and was better than what I had been given as a child. I can find comfort in that. We all can at least try to do better, to surpass and rise above the examples we were framed by. If you can't imagine ever having any better than the love you were given, then, my friend, how blessed you are. For you there is little excuse not to live an abundant life of sharing and giving to the fullest measure.

Later came the trouble with one of my children. My father was correct: my love ran deep. I was in trouble. The ropes had found my back again. This time the punches were coming fast and hard. Was it that I felt them more? I tried to counter. My timing was off. The fire I was returning was not well lit. Where was the strength? What happened? Why was I losing the fight? Round after round I attempted to fight on. Where was God? Why so much pain? I was working still, dealing with the patients in need. I was doing this while my own needs were going unmet.

At what point did I throw in the towel? Where was the sobriety? Financial ruin ensued. Abandonment. I lost faith. I did not lean on God or a higher power. I didn't trust. I relied on myself. I was not enough. The times of drunken cowardice. Searching and reaching out for love in the wrong places. The foul stench of defeat in the air and being left only with more pain and emptiness. In the end, it was just a pile of dung added to fuel the fire of a life without meaning. A life without God. Alone. Rejected. Given another name by friends who remained close, asking me to find myself among the rubble. Had I become Job? Some did call me that. There were no visible open wounds, but they were there just the same.

Oh my Lord. I cry out! I ask for mercy and forgiveness. I failed for a time. I wandered in the wilderness. I now realize that love was always there. It was a matter of depth and perception on my part.

My son is all right presently. He has come through his own anger to resolve. He's breathing without my air in his lungs. I am thankful for that. My girls are well, and love has found them. They give it in return. I made the movie. It hit at the wrong time for a return of money, it seems, but it gave me my chance to grieve. It gave me a chance to share the message with others. I reached out. God reached for me, and I felt him. He let me know he was still there. My legs are beneath me again. They are weak at times, but at least they bear up under the weight more often. I am fighting off of the ropes, not as physically strong but with renewed courage and strength of a different kind. I may not be restored in full, like Job, but it is coming—in this life or the next.

I am a better person. The fire burned me. Though scars may be reminders, I am full more often than before—full of love for others. I have taken a long look in the mirror. I like what I see again most of the time. Truthfully, more than ever. I may never be rich, but I am wealthy. I continue to care for my patients. I've drawn a line in the sand to enforce rules that make certain I am giving to those who have earned it. I am there for those truly in need. Patients who are discharged due to infractions and dishonesty fight back with negative physician reviews. It doesn't matter. I am doing the right thing. That's the only thing that matters.

In this book I shared topics of concern. This was not an attempt to discuss or resolve all of life's issues.

It remains more of a confession of a human life. Of the struggles that shape us. The wars that strip us. The love that forgives us. The love that erases regret. The love that's given despite feelings to the contrary. The love that frees us.

My dear friend, everything is relative. How much pain does each of us experience? How do we understand the problems of others when we have not endured them ourselves? Are there children dying of starvation? Is someone being raped or murdered while I am writing this? Surely. Some of us believe we have endured or suffered greatly, yet there are those who would give anything to trade places with each of us. What can we do? How do we return fire? With love whenever we can. It endures. It remains. It is all you will leave behind that will matter. It is the great equalizer. It is life in full measure.

Let go of anger. Bitterness, be quiet! Return to the depths of hell you came from. What else will I face before the final bell sounds? I shudder to think. Yet I can believe. I can choose. I can find love. With it I can fight on. I can counter. If I can, I believe you can as well.

When I began this effort, this writing, I questioned my motive. I even wondered if I would die when I hit the last key. I actually believed I would at one point. This is it. This is my testimony. This is my life. This is my epitaph. The last key is about to be struck. At this point I am still here. Will I write on? Will I live on? Each breath and moment is a gift from God. No matter. I will do it with love. Will you? I hope so.

> Love is the power that makes your heart beat
> It can make you move mountains, make you drop to your knees
> When it finally hits you, you won't know what to do
> There's nothin' you can say, when love finds you
>
> Give it all you can give it, when your love comes around
> If you put your heart in it, then it won't let you down
> You'll find out it's true, babe, someday when love finds you
> (Vince Gill, "When Love Finds You")

Here it is, Lord, my god of the universe. Here I am, broken while full. I am here, Lord. I believe. I know I am forgiven. I know I am blessed. I am not ashamed. I am a simple man. Of no consequence? Not much fame or glory here? No matter. The glory will come. I can love God. I can and I will. I promise. Unconditionally. See you soon, Tamara. You as well, Mom and Dad.

Thanks for the pain, God. It was a gift. Thank you for all of it. I am yours now. I can see. We are all going to die. How will we live? As you made clear, the greatest gift of all was here all along. It was love.

This is the story of my life at sixty plus. It has been said that if your story is not giving you what you want, then change your story. At least change your view of it. Ask yourself, what is the story behind the story? Life is happening for me and not to me. Do joy. Do happiness. As much as you can, for the alternative does not help. Live life on your terms. Do this by the manner in which you perceive what has happened, that it was for your good. It made you who you are. Do you like who you are? Don't let the heartache and agony be wasted. No one said it would be easy. I believe we are called to give our best. This is success. This is love!

The more I know, the less I understand...
I've been tryin' to get down to the heart of the matter
But my will gets weak
And my thoughts seem to scatter
But I think it's about forgiveness...
Ah, these times are so uncertain
There's a yearning undefined
And people filled with rage...
How can love survive in such a graceless age?
Oh, pride and competition
Cannot fill these empty arms...
There are people in your life
Who've come and gone
They let you down
You know they hurt your pride

You better put it all behind you baby…
You keep carryin' that anger
It'll eat you up inside, baby…
Because the flesh will get weak
And the ashes will scatter
So I'm thinkin' about forgiveness
(Don Henley, "The Heart of the Matter")

Maybe I have nothing to offer by the standards set in this world. I fought to gain material wealth. Why? So I might matter? So someone would love me? Others might think, there he is! Maybe he will sign a book for me. Perhaps this pride and ego are the main reasons I was never allowed to have fame or fortune. It is all right now. I understand. I get it. Am I alone now? Except for the love of the children and many friends, there are no tender mercies. No arms to hold me. Will they ever again? I have my doubts. It's just me and the universe. Lessons learned. I can love; therefore, I am. No, my friend, listen! You can hear it. You can feel it. It is the universe calling. We are not alone!

Please, God, the higher power, whoever you are. From me, the fighter, actor, writer, producer, musician, physician, officer, son, father, spouse, and more as well as less. From me, the unknown. This human who will likely return to dust with only a few who remember him. I am asking you with humility, tenderness, mercy, forgiveness, and a limited understanding of the eternity that awaits me, please, let someone read and be blessed by this letter. Let this person think of his or her life and what it means, how he or she will be remembered. Let this person love, I beg. Please, let him or her love!

"So hush little baby, don't you cry. You know your daddy's bound to die. But all my trials, Lord, will soon be over." (Elvis Presley, "An American Trilogy")

> I always meant to ask you about the war
> And what you saw across a bridge too far
> Did it leave a scar?
>
> Or how you navigated wings of fires and steel
> Up where heaven had no more secrets to conceal
> And still you found the ground beneath your wheels
> How did it feel?
>
> Bang the drum slowly, play the pipe lowly
> To dust be returning, from dust we begin
> Bang the drum slowly, I'll speak of things holy
> Above and below me, world without end...
>
> I meant to bring you water from the well
> And be the one beside you when you fell
> Could you tell?
> (Emmylou Harris, "Bang the Drum Slowly")

Oh God! Oh universe! Oh Lord of Lords! I have lived here. I have loved here. I have lost here. Money. Things. There was no stability found in this wandering soul.

What did I lose that was priceless, irreplaceable? It was faith, God. When I didn't understand, with arrogance I asked why? I demanded an answer, in this place between heaven and hell. Lost faith causes the loss of the most important thing of all: The greatest gift. The measure of all that remains. The only thing of consequence. I lost love. I humbly ask for it back, to show it as much as I can, to give it to those who will accept it.

I am ashamed, my God. Thank you for letting me see. I was not taught stability and have not lived much of it. It is not too late, God. It is not too late, universe. It is not too late to love. Help me. Let me. Forgive me. Yet I know. I understand. I was burned by pain. Yet you do love me. It is there. It always was, despite all that has happened. Whether negative or positive, not even knowing which, no matter my state or condition, let me go out loving.

Frankly, there are times when my will to fight is weak. My confidence has been weathered and torn. There are days when I am not sure what I have left. What is there to be of help to others, much less to myself? Is there yet time to heal from all the defeats? The ability to fight through another round? For those who can feel this pain, this loss, I say love can give us purpose, another chance, a reason to continue. No matter the situation—the past, the present, the future—there is hope. There can be renewed strength. There can be purpose. Love endures. Love connects me. It is the rule of one. Reach for the distant star. It is love that allows me to pass into eternity, where love is eternal. Love never fails.

Someone once told me, "Lynn, you are a legend in your own mind." I don't know where that came from. If I am a legend, it's for the loss of mind and the restrained reasoning that follows. I am certain misfortune fell upon me. I also remain confident my own insanity contributed to my demise. I struggled to remain within the shelter of love during tragedies but failed to do so. It is very simple, really, not as complex as I made out. We react and in doing so can rush blindly into deeper destruction. You, like me, may be left with a sense of great loss and loneliness. You are left to wonder why. You feel a sense of doom and despair, overwhelming thoughts of failure and regret, realizing that death is coming. Mistakes were many, and what value did I have? Why did I have to make something that was already hard even more difficult? Lean on this. There are people who are worse off and feel much the same. Reach out; they will be there. Love them. Leave love behind, and in doing so have faith that it is love never ending that awaits. I have helped make a mess of myself. I will do my best to take what is left and love.

I pray this book is published following my book *Days Gone By* and the movie I wrote and produced, *Heaven and Hell*. If given time, I pray, those who read or watch will be blessed by the common theme in all of them, the same theme that to this day follows me as I treat patients and remain a parent. Through it all, the only thing that mattered was love: that somewhere in the midst of despair and pain, there was room, a place in the heart reserved for love. Love isn't easy at times. I have shared more than enough excuses to choose hatred and bitterness.

As I mentioned some have known me well enough to refer to me as Job. Job was tested. God called him righteous. Though confused over the reasons for his torment, he accepted the will of a higher power. I asked, Why me? Why Tamara? Countless couples given years together were reminders of my loss. Job leaned not upon his own ability to understand. I didn't do that. I demanded an explanation. Therein lies a major difference. I had to learn the same. Through mercy and blood not of my own, I am forgiven. In that I am perfect. I did not hold on to my faith. I tried too hard to understand—a finite being attempting to comprehend an infinite universe. I was not righteous in and of myself, as clearly explained in this letter. I was not Job. I am simply Marvin.

I hurt myself today
To see if I still feel
I focus on the pain
The only thing that's real...

Try to kill it all away
But I remember everything

What have I become
My sweetest friend
Everyone I know
Goes away in the end

And you can have it all
My empire of dirt...

If I could start again
A million miles away
I will keep myself
I would find a way
(Nine Inch Nails, "Hurt")

I wanted to let others see that we are not alone. Your pain and confusion are felt by many others, both great and small by the world's standards. Some may have lived full lives while others ached with the beatings of emptiness. Some, perhaps, were blessed to experience few tragedies. Countless thousands were buried in the rubble of them, such as my own mother, who believed life was too painful to endure. She invited death. Yet I knew I could not inflict that upon my children, because there is *no love* in it.

There have been legends, presidents. After their deaths, we remember their journeys and what they stood for. Not all of us will be written about. But it doesn't matter. This life truly brings both joy and pain. The measure of us is how we deal with it. It is our legacy to choose love and not hate. Of course we have regrets. It is our task to embrace them as I mentioned, to have too few to remember. I know what it is like to drown in them. I believe our best chance is to get up each day and choose love. That can be the great eraser. Take a deep breath. Choose to finish strong. It is not easy. I still fail. I make the effort, however.

Friends, lovers, and family: for the good, the bad, the ugly, even if from a safe distance, choose love. Decide to remember the good. Hatred and swallowing the pill of bitterness serve no good to anyone. To live by the sword is to die by it. Be merciful. Abide in love. Each of us has a story, a journey. Allow your legacy to be love. Many have suffered while living more than I did. Surely some have not. Let us cling to love. If eternity is truly full and measured by infinite love, then living love should prepare us for it. I have fought the arrows of bitterness only to be defeated by them. It should be obvious it did not serve me well.

I am not famous. People read many works because of recognition. I am yet to be recognized. But what does that matter? I am a commoner, like many of you—a nobody to many, perhaps a loser or fool to others. Not all of us will make a great mark while we are here. Some will die under the blankets of their own despair. Our journeys don't have to remain meaningless, however. Love can turn a nobody into somebody. If I was a fool, let it be for love. At the least, my cause was noble. Strive to show love to someone daily. It will change his or her day. It will mean the day was not wasted. It did not fail for a lack of love. After all, isn't it said to be the greatest gift of all? As tired as I am, I do make the effort to show love to someone each day.

> Growing older now
> Where did we learn to worry from?
> Why does fear stop anyone?
> We've become afraid
> Try to fill the void inside our soul
> In the end it's our love that made the day
> Through the good and bad
> We can make it OK
> Remember where we started in the first place!
> Just stay
> (Taylor and Ali Faulkner, "Just Stay")

If I die soon—and there have been times when I considered that I might—let someone read my *Letter to God*. I am coming home, Lord. Let there be love. Let this letter give people hope when all else is lost. It is me, God. I am living out the end of my days, a victim of myself. I will make every effort to finish as I should: a soldier of love. I will be coming home soon, to meet you at last, to see family and friends I loved while they were here. I suppose I learned the hard way. Children, have a better understanding of your earthly father. There is another, one much greater. That greater infinite being will not fail. Why? Because of love.

I had much go wrong. Reason and sanity left me. I have nothing. I am empty, so much in need of forgiveness. Yet I may have found everything. It was simple all along. I did not fail. In the end there was love. Because of this love, let me and those who embrace this testament have what I promised: to not fear death. Let death come when it comes. Let love remain and endure on into eternity! Let us die well and in doing so live as we never have.

Let me paraphrase Hemingway: There is no shame in being a broken man. Life can break every one of us. The good, the kind, the brave. Those it doesn't break, it can kill. Let me now take this further. Love can save the broken. It can deal with the shame. It can let kindness be kinder still, let the good be better still, let the brave be more courageous than ever. Pain will not kill you, but it will allow you to fully live, now and forever.

Love is dancing all around you. *Love and Fear* do not abide together or ever embrace. Therefore, don't be afraid. Just dance. Dance with love! It is a daily task. Nothing is easy here. It wasn't intended to be. Yet when we love, we shine. We rise above defeat and misery. Though we are weary, we fly and soar on the wings of eagles. This is what love does. This is our destiny and what defines us. Love! It is me, God. Thank you for everything. I look forward to meeting you. I did as you asked. I asked others to consider it as well. I chose well. I recently had a patient who told me about a year ago I made all the difference in her life. Naturally I asked what I had done. She indicated I had given her a hug and told her I loved her.

Now you know. You are not alone. Others have had tragedy fall on them hard. Others have made a complete mess of things. Love can clean it up. Listen to me. Without love I had nothing. Nothing at all. It is all there is. The only thing that makes life worth living—enduring, everlasting, the beginning and the end, the end that is a new beginning. Like me, if you made a mess here and there, or if you believe everything has gone bad for the most part, where is the cleanup? Where is the meaning you were searching for? What difference will your life make? Your death? You can find it in love. *Madness* is everywhere. Love is not madness. Choose love!

Everything I shared was not for me alone. It was for us together. I have hung my life on a cross, an account of the good, bad, and ugly within one life. It is to encourage you to do the same. In doing so, conclude how important it is to love. Do not be afraid.

A new command I give you: love one another.
As I have loved you, so you must love one
another.

—Jesus Christ

What you leave behind is not what is engraved
in stone monuments, but what is woven into
the lives of others.

—Pericles

*The choices we make are the only
thing we own.*

—*Between Heaven and Hell*

I have lived in the country. Lived in the suburbs. Resided in the concrete city. Mingled with the entitled. Treated all types. Sat with the homeless on a bench. Worked with and for the talented yet humble, as well as the arrogant. Placed money in the jar of the unknown guitar player and singer. Searched for evidence of love and kindness.

I had some talent myself, enough that I thought about many different paths of direction regarding life and choices. I looked for inspiration to write with passion and depth about the journey. I have concluded that my wandering soul and open heart revealed I was at home with the homeless. This was so because of love. Light up the darkness! Listen to Beethoven. Love ran from him. Even so, his greatest work reflected the love near the end of his life: "Ode to Joy."

With love,
Marvin

ABOUT THE AUTHOR

About Dr. Marvin Faulkner

If there is anyone who could testify to the commonplace expression, "no pain, no gain," it is Dr. Marvin Faulkner, D.O. The double board certified anesthesiologist and pain management physician has not only witnessed and treated the many facets of his patients' physical pain, he has personally lived through many layers of personal pain for decades. A former wrestling and Golden Glove boxing champion, he early on experienced the throb of intense training and stepping in and out of the ring. However, that discomfort only scratched the surface of the stinging emotional and psychological heartache that cut deeper than any punch ever thrown, as he experienced tragedy after tragedy in his life and in the lives of the people closest to him.

That this pain has made him stronger is an understatement and his story is an incredible testament to the power of faith, hope, and love. *Letter To God: A Memoir-Transcending Pain through the Power of Love.* Dr. Faulkner's second book, following *Days Gone By: Reflecting on Life's Meaning with Humor & Hope*, a witty account about dealing with life's struggles with a good dose of healing laughter and plenty of lessons learned. His first written work was the screenplay, *Between Heaven and Hell,* for which he also produced the independent film and starred as its lead role.

Dr. Faulkner currently resides in Kansas City, Mo., where he continues to help others with pain management — both through his medical practice and his written words.

Made in the USA
Lexington, KY
14 September 2019